JEFFREY TUCKER
— SECOND EDITION —

Liberty

Lockdown

Foreword by George Gilder

BROWNSTONE INSTITUTE

Liberty or Lockdown
By Jeffrey Tucker

Second edition copyright © 2022 Brownstone Institute (Austin, Texas),
Creative Commons Attribution International 4.0. Originally published
2020 by The American Institute for Economic Research,
Creative Commons Attribution International 4.0.

Physical ISBN: 9781630695934
Digital ISBN: 9781630695927

Design: Vanessa Mendozzi

JEFFREY TUCKER

— SECOND EDITION —

Liberty

Lockdown

Foreword by George Gilder

BROWNSTONE
INSTITUTE

CONTENTS

The Choice

The Carnage

The History

The Hope

New Introduction

The significance of the timing of the first edition of this book is obvious to anyone who has lived through our strange times: September 2020. That was six months following the lockdown of most of the world during which places where people might "congregate" were shut by governments. The reason was to avoid, mitigate, eliminate maybe, or otherwise diminish the disease impact of the virus that caused Covid. This was before the vaccine came out, before the Great Barrington Declaration, and before data on excess deaths the world over showed vast carnage from these policy decisions.

The state was unleashed on the population as never before, in the name of science. There are no words to describe my outrage then and now.

The onset of lockdowns put me to work trying to understand the thinking, a process which took me back through the history of pandemics, the relationship between infectious disease and freedom, and the origin of lockdown ideology in 2005.

The times during which this book was written were beyond strange. People went full medieval in every way in which that term can be understood. There was public flogging in the form of masking and the abolition of fun, feudalistic segregation and disease shaming, the practical end of most medical care unless it was for Covid, the scapegoating of non-compliers, the neglect and abuse of children, and a turn to other pre-modern forms. All of this became worse once the non-sterilizing vaccines appeared on the market that many if not most people were forced to accept at pains of losing their jobs.

Writing now September 2022, I cannot even imagine going through the pain of putting this research together again. I'm very pleased it was done then because now this book survives as a marker that there was dissent, if nothing else. I've added no new essays though I've written hundreds since then. The second edition should really stand as is.

This was also a period of time – still is today – when vast numbers of people feel betrayed by technology, media, politicians, and even their one-time intellectual heroes. It is a time of grave destruction with still-broken supply chains, roaring inflation, mass cultural demoralization, labor market confusions, shattered lives of young and old, and terrible uncertainty about the future.

When I put this book to bed in 2020, I had hoped we were near the end of this disaster. How wrong I was! Let us hope, too, that it is a period of rebuilding, however quietly it is taking place. Starting Brownstone Institute is part of that for me. So many others have joined. Today we published articles from all over the world since so many around the world have shared in this suffering. What will it take to emerge from the other side? From my point of view, it is not complicated. We need a renewed appreciation of human liberty and rights. That's it. That is the whole prescription. It does not sound hard but apparently it is. This task will likely consume the rest of our lives.

JEFFREY TUCKER

September 2022

Foreword by George Gilder

By late April 2020, with reports of plummeting death rates from all causes, the Covid-19 crisis was already essentially over. Signs mounted that this "viral new mania," as I called it, was far less severe than previous flus in 1918, 1958, and 1968 that occasioned no lockdowns or business closures despite millions of deaths from each around the globe. With the average age of Covid-19 deaths reported to be as high as 85 in Massachusetts where I reside and look on in wild surmise, the real mortality numbers for Covid-19 sunk into the statistical noise.

Hey, but why am I telling you this, when you hold in your hand this stirring and authoritative work by the eminent Jeffrey Tucker who has mastered all the data and transcended it with a redemptive call to sanity and real science?

With deaths from Covid-19 coming at an age higher than the age of normal deaths and the crisis evidently defunct, a new pandemic of doom erupted as a panic of pols. In rising astonishment, we contemplate a comedy of mash-minded med admins and stooges, covering their ifs, ands, and butts with ever more morbid and distorted statistics.

By September, the Centers for Disease Control (CDC) acknowledged that only six percent of US deaths came from Covid-19 alone. The average number of comorbidities such as diabetes or cancer was 2.6. Thus definitive Covid-19 deaths (caused by the coronavirus alone) had only reached a US total of some 10,000 by the end of the summer, less than ordinary flu which takes many more young people.

As deaths plummeted, governors seized ever more extreme emergency powers. Testing their citizens prodigally, they obsessively counted positives as "cases." As Tucker understands, the positives are increasingly statistical "false positives" since the vast majority of the test takers are free of the disease. Accompanied by no symptoms, this became a disease so fearful in its effects that you could not tell that you had it.

The country broke into two, with mostly "slave states" in the North and Far West fraught with masks and lockdowns, and free states in the South, such as Georgia, Florida, and Texas where Governors refused to take a "hammer and sickle" to their economies.

The crisis chiefly hit the politicians and the political Doctor Fauci who had gullibly accepted and trumpeted what statistician William Briggs called "the most colossal and costly blown forecast of all time."[1]

An egregious statistical horror story of millions of projected deaths, suffused with incense and lugubrious accents from Imperial College of London to Harvard School of Public Health, prompted the pols to impose a vandalistic lockdown on the economy. It would have been an outrage even if the assumptions were not wildly astronomically wrong.

Flattening the curve was always a fool's errand that widened the damage.

Already in April, a global study published in Israel by Professor Isaac Ben-Israel, chairman of the Israeli Space Agency and Council on Research and Development, showed that "the spread of the coronavirus declines to almost zero after 70 days—no matter where it strikes, and no matter what measures governments impose to try to thwart it."[2]

This study's conclusions were repeatedly confirmed in the months that followed, as Jeffrey Tucker documents in this profound and incendiary book. He covers the onset of the lockdowns, the outrageous political response, the psychological and medical toll, the immense economic costs, the history of 20th century viruses and the political response, and so much more, including and especially the irresponsible media coverage that helped fuel and cover up the political panic.

As he shows, this virus like all previous viral flus will give way only to herd immunity and to the natural immunity of most human beings to the worst effects. Whether through natural propagation of an extremely

---

1 Briggs, William M. 2020. "Coronavirus Update X: Juicing The Numbers, Prolonging The Pain." *William M. Briggs*, April 14.

2 Ben-Israel, Isaac. 2020. "The end of exponential growth: The decline in the spread of coronavirus." *The Times of Israel*, April 19.

infectious pathogen, or through the success of one of the hundreds of vaccine projects, or through the mutation of the virus to ubiquitous predictability like the common cold, the virus will become a trivial event.

In the meantime, no evidence indicates that this virus was exceptionally dangerous except in nursing homes and prisons densely populated with already vulnerable people. On March 20, 2020, the French published a major controlled study that shows no excess mortality at all from coronavirus compared to other flus. SARS and Mers were both much more lethal and did not occasion the destruction of the economy, the arts, and normal life.

We now know that the crisis was a comedy of errors. The Chinese evidently let it get going in the raw bat markets of Wuhan. But together with the Koreans, the Chinese dithered and demurred and allowed six weeks of rampant propagation to create herd immunity before they began locking everyone up. Therefore, the Chinese and Koreans were among the first to recover.

The Italians scared everybody with their haphazard health system and smoking fogies. Crammed together in subways and tenements, the New Yorkers registered a brief blip of extreme cases. Intubations and ventilators pushed down people's throats turned out not to help (80 percent died). This sowed fear and frustration among medical personnel slow to see that the problem was impaired hemoglobin in the blood rather than lung damage.

The New York media piled on with panic, with bogus reports of rising deaths. "Coronavirus deaths" soared by assuming that people dying with the virus were dying from it and then by ascribing to the coronavirus other deaths among people with symptoms of pulmonary distress, even without being tested.

The death rate rises with further reclassification of pneumonia and other pulmonary deaths. When we reach herd immunity, and nearly everyone has the antigen, nearly all deaths can be chalked up to Covid-19. It can become *Quod Erat Demonstrandum* for the panic mongers.

In a fascinating open letter to German Prime Minister Angela Merkel, epidemiologist Sucharit Bhakti concludes that with the French study, corroborated by findings from a Stanford antibody seroprevalence study in Santa Clara County, "the case for extreme measures collapses like a house of cards." Bhakti says that since the virus has already spread widely in the general population, efforts to stop further spread are both futile and destructive.

So let's stop pretending that our policies have been rational and need to be phased out, as if they once had a purpose. They should have been reversed summarily in March and acknowledged to be a mistake, perpetrated by statisticians with erroneous computer models. Instead we were subject to six months of hell, all beautifully documented by Tucker.

Another dramatic failure in 2020 traces to the failure of the intellectual classes to speak out. The civil libertarians went quiet. The center-left became full pro-lockdown, mostly likely for political reasons, regardless of the cost.

Somehow, to be pro-lockdown became an orthodoxy. Dissidents feared for their jobs and reputations. Suddenly in these days, to have favored normal life and freedom of association became a thought crime.

Which is why Jeffrey Tucker became such a crucial voice. Even in January 2020, before the rest of the world seemed to notice what was occuring in China, he was urging that we respond to this virus through medical and not political means. The world should have listened. With Tucker's book available, we have a soaring and searing plea never to do this again.

It's liberty or lockdown. We have to choose.

GEORGE GILDER

Introduction

For most Americans, the Covid-19 lockdown was our first experience in a full denial of freedom. Businesses forced closed. Schools, padlocked. Church, same. Theaters, dead. We were told to stay home, risking fines if we leave and jail if we don't pay. We couldn't travel. Separated from loved ones. This job is essential, this one is not. This surgery is cancelled, this one is not. You want a visitor from abroad? Forget it. The neighboring state? Only with a two-week quarantine.

Our world was, in a seeming instant, conspicuously divided between the rule makers and the rule followers, and what those rules would be felt completely arbitrary but strictly enforced. All our civic clichés about freedom, democracy, bravery, and rights were made null and void.

We were forced to spend day after day under effective house arrest, spinning aimlessly in this small and unwelcome world of captivity, wondering about big things previously unconsidered: why has this happened to me, what has gone wrong, why am I here, when will it end, what are my goals, what is the purpose of my life?

It was a transformation for all of us. The darkness came upon us suddenly, even though in the first two weeks of March 2020, we all sensed that something dramatic was happening. The perils of the virus were enough to strike fear but we also knew that in these hyper-political times, a disease would not be regarded as a matter to be addressed between patient and doctor. It would be up to the decisions of the people who happened to be holding power at the time, along with their advisors.

There would be some political response, some test of state powers, though to what extent and what form, we knew not. We could not have imagined in those days that the whole population would come to be subjected to a sadistic social experiment in the name of virus mitigation.

We could not have imagined that the whole of the freedoms and rights we had previously taken for granted – choice of leisure, dining, travel, profession, and education – would be taken from us in a matter of days, and only given back slowly over six months (or more).

During those times, we found ourselves controlled by a new social protocol while giving voice to a new and strange language. Forced human separation was given the oxymoronic label "social distancing." Brutal business closures were called "Targeted Layered Containment" (TLC, which in the American lexicon once meant "tender loving care"). House arrest was rechristened as a "Non-Pharmaceutical Intervention." We were all made part of an experimental game, encouraged to see ourselves as bit players on bell-shaped curves we needed to help flatten and viral spreads we needed to slow.

We suffered to reduce suffering. We sacrificed to minimize sacrifice. We were banned from gyms for our health, prevented from entering houses of worship for our own edification, stopped from working so that our overlords could do their work on a virus they couldn't see, and prevented from travelling to stop population movements so that medical professionals could better test, track, and trace us.

What were we allowed to do? Find a new way, without much of what we used to do, such as see friends, hang out downtown, make choices, go here and there. Instead, just watch television. Gorge on old movies since all new releases were stopped. Do video calls. Make quick store runs provided you came right back home. The right to attend a funeral, go to the office, get your teeth cleaned, host a party, go to the beach, buy some shoes, hang a drink at your favorite watering hole, take a trip – it was all suddenly illegal. Our choices were throttled and our lives scripted in the name of public health.

The children, what happened to them? The managerial elite scrapped everything they knew about their lives. All that parents took for granted, all for which they already paid, came to an end. The students, what happened to them? They were locked out of their dorms and told to learn online.

The people with everything to gain from the lockdowns had nothing to lose; the people who had nothing to gain lost everything.

Even as I write, with hints of Autumn in the air, we can't go to the movies, walk indoors without masks, hold larger parties, or attend events.

And it's not just governments and police we fear but even more so the sternly earnest enforcers among the citizenry, even more zealous than the Centers for Disease Control, itching to report all dissidents to the health police. And for what? Wearing a mask on the chin instead of the mouth, or just on the mouth rather than the nose too, or perhaps for engaging in criminal activity such as walking backwards on a one-way grocery aisle.

I've been writing about pandemics and liberty for 15 years. I knew from 2005 that there were plans in place for mass quarantines. I knew from 2006 that there were fanatics out there who imagined that they could use the power of the state to suppress a virus by suppressing our freedoms. The plans were on the shelf and I wrote to warn that it was conceptually possible. Even so, I really never imagined that such would be tried.

Why and how did it happen?

The why turns out to have little if anything to do with the known and settled science on matters of viruses and their mitigation. The prevailing policy ethos that hit us in early March 2020 was borrowed from the most primitive impulses last operational in the Middle Ages: a disease is a miasma from which we must run and hide. Another was from the ancient world: presume everyone is carrying a deadly pathogen. By everyone, I mean, truly. Even children who have near zero susceptibility. Another pre-modern virus practice of our time is basically borrowed from grade-school myths about "cooties" (called "lurgy" in the UK).

These base superstitions were packaged up and delivered unto us all by a highly irresponsible media apparatus hungry for clicks and mind share, and then given the cover of science by the new kids on the epide-miological block: the agent-based modelers. Somehow all law, philosophy, tradition, economics, and even all other medicine, bowed before their wild computer-based projections of mass death. But, they told us, there was a path toward preventing one in six of your friends from dying. You must be locked down and live under their stern rule with governors, prime ministers, mayors, and presidents as their handmaidens.

There were dissidents, top minds from the medical research profession, people with powerful curriculum vitae and prestige positions. Incredibly, their videos were often pulled by the tech giants for violating terms of service. We were dangerously close to achieving full censorship of dissidents. The more implausible the basis for the destruction of our lives the tighter the controls became on the information we could receive.

The politicians panicked. They feared being blamed for any and all deaths from this one virus while forgetting other ailments. The Covid-19 fear drove out every other consideration. It was madness but it was only supposed to last a couple of weeks until it turned out to last six months and longer.

Why didn't we revolt? Part of the reason was that most of us were in shock. We had to believe that there was some good reason, some rationale, for these policies. But as the weeks and months rolled on, the terrible truth began to dawn on more people. This was all for naught. We destroyed the country, and much of the world, and everything people had worked hard for centuries to build, to try out something that had never been tried before. It didn't work. The virus took its own path. And today we are left with this wreckage.

As I type today (September 1, 2020), I'm feeling ever vindicated by the research, and ever more optimistic that we are going to get through this, the world will open up again, and we can begin the rebuilding. The work that is before us is not only national, institutional, and economic. It is also psychological. Our lives have been shattered in incredible ways.

We are not the first to go through this. It is something experienced by prisoners, and by previous populations under lockdown. During the worst of the lockdowns, I took comfort in reading – over and over – Albert Camus's classic and astonishingly brilliant book *The Plague* from 1947.[3] There is a chapter that describes the inner life of people who have experienced lockdown for the first time. It came suddenly in the presence of a deadly disease. The entire town of 200,000 closed. No one in or out.

It's fiction but all-too-real. Reading it slowly and nearly out loud is an experience. The poetry of the prose is incredible, but more so the depth of knowledge of the inner workings of the mind.

> One of the most striking consequences of the closing of the gates was, in fact, this sudden deprivation befalling people who were

---

3 Camus, Albert. 1947. *The Plague*. Random House, Inc.: US. Available for read and download from Archive.org.

completely unprepared for it. [...] This drastic, clean-cut depri-
vation and our complete ignorance of what the future held in
store had taken us unawares; we were unable to react against the
mute appeal of presences, still so near and already so far, which
haunted us daylong. [...T]he plague forced inactivity on them,
limiting their movements to the same dull round inside the
town, and throwing them, day after day, on the illusive solace of
their memories. For in their aimless walks they kept on coming
back to the same streets and usually, owing to the smallness of
the town, these were streets in which, in happier days, they had
walked with those who now were absent.

And then we realized that the separation was destined to
continue, we had no choice but to come to terms with the
days ahead. In short, we returned to our prison-house, we had
nothing left us but the past, and even if some were tempted
to live in the future, they had speedily to abandon the idea—
anyhow, as soon as could be—once they felt the wounds that
the imagination inflicts on those who yield themselves to it.

[...] At such moments the collapse of their courage, willpower,
and endurance was so abrupt that they felt they could never
drag themselves out of the pit of despond into which they had
fallen. Therefore they forced themselves never to think about
the problematic day of escape, to cease looking to the future,
and always to keep, so to speak, their eyes fixed on the ground
at their feet. [...] Thus, in a middle course between these heights
and depths, they drifted through life rather than lived, the prey
of aimless days and sterile memories, like wandering shadows
that could have acquired substance only by consenting to root
themselves in the solid earth of their distress[...]

Hostile to the past, impatient of the present, and cheated
of the future, we were much like those whom men's justice, or
hatred, forces to live behind prison bars.

How do we come back from this? By reflecting, learning, and acting
on the promise of renewal. It can happen, but only once we fully come to

terms with the stark choice between liberty and lockdown. Liberty is right and it works. Lockdown is wrong and it does not. It's not complex but it takes courage and determination to live out that principle. The United States was founded on the principle of liberty as a right. We must reclaim that. We must work to take away lockdown discretionary power from our leaders. And we must reclaim confidence and hope in the future.

This book is assembled from my writings over these past months, placed in an ordering that makes sense, and edited to update the information. They cover history, politics, economics, and the relevant science as it pertains, and especially on this latter topic I've been very careful to rely on the expertise of others from whom I've learned so much.

They were all published by the American Institute for Economic Research (AIER), which found itself in the position of being a major distributor of research and critical analysis of the greatest government-caused crisis in our lifetimes. AIER was perfectly positioned to do this but I must tell you that it has not been easy. We've been subjected to denunciation, censorship, shaming, threats and even worse, from people who didn't believe there should be any dissent.

It's a wonderful thing to work as Editorial Director at AIER, and my debt to my colleagues is incalculable: Edward Stringham, Peter C. Earle, Phillip Magness, Alexander Gleason, Micha Gartz, Thomas Hogan, Brad DeVos, Patricia Areano, Robert Wright, Daniel Klein, Sharni Cutajar, Stephen Miller, Joakim Book, David Schatz, Art Carden, Richard Ebeling, Donald Boudreaux, Veronique de Rugy, Charles Cole, Ethan Yang, Fiona Harrigan, David Waugh, Vincent Geloso, Jennifer Nuzzo, Knut Wittkowski, Raymond Niles, Robert Hughes, Lucio Eastman, Roger Koops, Jason Kelly, Taleed Brown, George Gilder, Stacey Rudin, Richard Salsmann, Alexander Salter, the many Twitter accounts that have been so fantastic in researching and disseminating credible information, the heroic academics who pressed on with credible research throughout, and the whole team of AIER and all those who work with us as partners in this great mission.

One more very special person is in my mind now: Warren Smith (1946-2020). He began to correspond with me with enthusiastic encouragement of my writings. His notes meant so much to me, and it was he who encouraged me to assemble this book, and then he even gave a generous contribution to AIER to make it possible. His last note to me was from the ICU unit of the hospital. The next correspondence came from his daughter who informed me of his death. It touched me deeply, and I knew then that I must complete the task. It is to Warren Smith and his memory that I dedicate this book.

The virus will vanish from the public mind as viruses do: inauspiciously as our clever immune systems incorporate its properties into our internal resistance codes. But we will have another struggle facing us in the years ahead concerning what precisely we are going to tolerate from our state officials and how much of a priority we are going to place on retaining our rights and liberties. This choice is something we must all face in our own lives, and then work to see instantiated in the legal structures of societies we hope can maintain their freedom.

The Choice

An Epistemic Crisis

This pandemic crisis was not only ever about health and economics; at the very onset of this pandemic, we experienced an epistemic meltdown. The core question concerned: knowledge. Information. Accurate information. How deadly was this? What were the risks? How did one become infected? The demographics of fatalities? The geography of the spread? How contagious, how deadly, how could we know, and how could we find out? Who could we trust with such wildly divergent opinions out there?

The information chaos began in January 2020, with films pouring out of Wuhan, China, with hazmatted police dragging people from their apartments and throwing them into quarantine. It all looked terrifying. People weren't panicked yet. Mostly, the media was trying to keep people calm.

In early March 2020, *Psychology Today* ran a piece on why we shouldn't panic.[4] "It's scary to think that an invisible enemy is out there to make you sick. But your doctor is not panicking, and you don't need to, either." The center left publication *Slate* said the same "COVID-19's Mortality Rate Isn't As High As We Think." "Don't hoard masks and food. Figure out how to help seniors and the immunosuppressed stay healthy," said the article.[5] Anthony Fauci told the *USA Today* that the risk posed by Covid-19 was "miniscule."[6]

---

4 Escalante, Alison. 2020. "Why Your Doctor Is Not Panicking about the Novel Coronavirus," *Psychology Today,* March 2.

5 Faust, Jeremy Samuel. 2020. "COVID-19's Mortality Rate Isn't As High As We Think," *Slate*, March 4.

6 O'Donnell, Jayne. 2020. "Top disease official: Risk of coronavirus in USA is 'miniscule;' skip mask and wash hands," *USA Today*, February 17.

Everyone was doing their best poring over the data we had and could access thanks to digital media, websites such as *OurWorldinData* and *Worldometer*, simply because the government's official page at the CDC did not provide enough data and its employees apparently took off for the weekend.[7] Based on what we saw, the infection rates were falling, defying the direst predictions. But the data were incomplete: testing was not universal, incubation rates were uncertain (5 to 14 days), and data in general relied on collection, which is itself an unscientific enterprise.

But think about the following. Above all else, the number one question people had in the early days of this crisis was: do I have the coronavirus? This more than anything else was the central concern. Remarkably, Americans did not know and had no means of finding out. The reason is now clear: the Centers for Disease Control had previously nationalized all disease testing. A government bureaucracy like any other. It's hardly surprising that it completely flopped.

A private researcher, funded by the Bill & Melinda Gates Foundation, was forcibly prevented from producing and distributing a valid test.[8] The CDC said no. More details rolled in about how all this went down, thanks to intrepid reporters who smelled a rat. The CDC in the first week of February 2020, sent 160,000 tests to labs around the country. The tests were faulty and produced confusing results. They were withdrawn, just as private laboratories fixed the test.

Still, no approval was being given for private labs to produce tests. For the very curious, you can read the many stories of private labs who were begging for a chance to do something about the problem.[9] The red tape, confusion, power struggles, and information blockages are being

---

7 Ritchie, Hannah, Esteban Ortiz-Ospina, Diana Beltekian, Edouard Mathieu, Joe Hasell et al. 2020. "Coronavirus Pandemic (COVID-19)." *Our World In Data*; CDC. 2020. "Cases in the U.S." *Centres for Disease Control and Prevention (CDC)*.

8 Thierer, Adam. 2020. "How the US Botched Coronavirus Testing." *American Institute for Economic Research*, March 12.

9 Baird, Robert P. 2020. "What Went Wrong with Coronavirus Testing in the U.S." *The New Yorker*, March 16.

documented by the day.[10] The *Washington Post* reports:[11]

> The US efforts to distribute a working test stalled until Feb. 28, when federal officials revised the CDC test and began loosening up FDA rules that had limited who could develop coronavirus diagnostic tests.

The CDC/FDA bans on private tests were done in the name of health and safety. That was the period in which panic enveloped the nation. No one knew. We had no means to find out. Everyone and everything flipped out. We replaced knowledge with panic and insanity, mostly due to the lack of information.

F.A. Hayek was right that the use of knowledge in society is the central issue in economic and social organization. We had been cut off from the knowledge flow that otherwise would have been ours had we left this issue entirely to the private sector, which would have brought a coronavirus test to you as quickly as you can order a pizza. Instead, there was nothing but confusion.[12]

> Shortly after Feb. 28, when CDC officials announced the decision to reconfigure the CDC test, the number of those tests run by public health labs soared, from roughly 25 or fewer per day to as many as 1,500. At the same time, authorities were allowing other facilities to use their own tests — including Cleveland Clinic, Stanford and Greninger's at the University of Washington.
>
> Even so, complaints of testing scarcity continued to roll in.. As tests become more widely available, experts and officials have cautioned that a backlog will continue because of critical

10 Khazan, Olga. 2020. "The 4 Key Reasons the U.S. Is So Behind on Coronavirus Testing." *The Atlantic*, March 13.

11 Whoriskey, Peter, and Neena Satija. 2020. "How U.S. coronavirus testing stalled: Flawed tests, red tape and resistance to using the millions of tests produced by the WHO." *The Washington Post*, March 16.

12 Whoriskey and Satija (2020).

shortages: swabs to collect patient samples, machines to extract the genetic material from the swabs, workers qualified to run the tests.

Even if those problems are resolved, however, those critical early delays, when the CDC was struggling to issue tests to the states, significantly damaged efforts to contain the spread of the coronavirus, experts said.

In a CDC tele-briefing on Feb. 29 that included some local and state public health directors, local officials lamented the initial inability to test. A reporter asked: "Did the lack of testing capabilities delay finding out who these cases were, particularly the person who died?"

In answering, Jeff Duchin, the public health chief in King County, Wash., where 37 deaths have been reported, suggested the lack of tests was critical, in addition to the fact that authorities had limited who could be tested. Initially, they had said tests would only be used for those who had traveled in affected regions of the globe or had otherwise been in contact with an infected person.

Another report adds:[13]

The void created by the CDC's faulty tests made it impossible for public-health authorities to get an accurate picture of how far and how fast the disease was spreading. In hotspots like Seattle, and probably elsewhere, COVID-19 spread undetected for several weeks, which in turn only multiplied the need for more tests.

Lacking that knowledge, public officials freaked out. Stay home. Keep your distance. Everyone is a suspect. Anyone and everyone could be positive for Covid-19. Socially shame anyone out and about. Silent

---

13 Baird, Robert P. 2020. "What Went Wrong with Coronavirus Testing in the U.S." *The New Yorker*, March 16.

spreaders are everywhere. Board up the bars![14] It was this sense, along with utter panic on the part of public officials, that led the markets to crash. After all, you can't have an economy if people cannot engage and trade, can't go to work, can't distribute goods and services, and forget about investment.

And here we find the key to understanding why this coronavirus produced a social and economic calamity, whereas the H1N1 (Swine flu) from ten years ago is barely remembered by most people. It came and went with a large health cost (infections: 57 million; fatalities 12,469) but low cost otherwise. The critical difference was that the CDC worked with private laboratories and medical facilities to get the test out there. A few public schools closed for part of the day but there was no panic, no large economic loss.

In the midst of all of this, this panic learning and trying, this speculation and searching, this mass national confusion, this endless and chaotic longing to know, this constant grasping for intelligence, one thing became certain: states at all levels decided to act. As if they knew the right course. And they acted with extreme force. And their message was always the same: stop whatever you are doing and do nothing instead. This was and is the ultimate expression of nihilism, the chaos that follows ignorance. Officials in this country decided to shut down society – as if this were even possible – as a replacement for reliable, usable, actionable knowledge that we were all forcibly prevented from gaining when we most needed it.

It's a classic pretension of knowledge about which the government itself is clueless. They tried to plan without reliable signs or signals. That's a recipe for chaotic, hasty, haphazard, and internally contradictory policy decisions, all driven by the need to maintain the appearance of an official response. Such circumstances are ripe for abuse. Contrary perspectives, such as that offered by Stanford bio-statistician John P.A. Ioannidis, were ignored.[15] In his view, we had absolutely no basis to assume that any

---

14 Woods, Amanda. 2020. "Cincinnati police board up bar that defied coronavirus shutdown order." *New York Post*, March 17.

15 Ioannidis, John P.A. 2020. "A fiasco in the making? As the coronavirus pandemic takes hold, we are making decisions without reliable data." *Stat News*, March 17.

existing models were right, and that the fatality rate could be extremely low (0.025%). Were these views ignored because he didn't have the right conclusion?

We got censorship of the problem when it first emerged, and then other governments were trying to cover their own rears for chaotic inaction. Then all the vultures arrived, trying to append their pet political projects to the response: authoritarian busybodies like Andrew Cuomo and New York Mayor Bill de Blasio instinctually called out the police or called for nationalization of industry, Bernie Sanders used it to make the case for Medicare for All, the UBI crowd tried to build that into a stimulus, the nationalists demanded a shutdown of global trade.

Then there was a huge debate in this country about how bad corona-virus really was. Some people were saying that we were all going to be infected. Many would die. Others were saying that this was completely overwrought, that authorities had overreacted, and that the virus would burn itself out and that the casualties would be relatively few and focused on those with low life expectancy. The problem was that we didn't have access to reliable, scientifically valid information either to avoid panic or behave in a rational way.

The contrast with South Korea, where infections had fallen and fallen, was striking.[16] There were no shutdowns, no geographic quarantines, no panics. Society was open for business. Life went on as normal but for one thing: people had access to testing, which is to say that people were given access to the essential and most important piece of information that was necessary at the time. The same was true in Sweden, which pursued an open policy even without much testing: officials worked to calm the public.

That was not the case in the US.

And that was a major source of the problem. The information problem turned out to be critical for the survival of economic life, exactly as F.A. Hayek discovered in the 20th century.[17] Those information flows, when

---

16 Earle, Peter C. 2020. "South Korea Preserved the Open Society and Now Infection Rates are Falling." *American Institute for Economic Research*, March 12.

17 Hayek, Friedrich A. 1945. "The Use of Knowledge in Society." *The Library of Economics and Liberty*.

they are cut off by force, for whatever reason, and in whatever form, lead to chaos. A tragic and deeply damaging chaos.

The knowledge gap came to be replaced by a howling media apparatus, which discovered between the end of February and the middle of March that the virus could be used for political purposes against its *bête noire* in the White House. Thus the virus became heavily political, departing from a long tradition in the United States that regarded disease as a medical matter only. What followed was six months of screaming, protesting, denouncing, and torrents of hate online and off.

After all this time, where stands the issue of testing? The chaos seemed to abate until it had not. The *New York Times* explained what several specialists had already explained to me in private. The PCR test for Covid-19 does not give clean 'yes' or 'no' answers. It all depends on the settings on the test itself. "On Thursday, the United States recorded 45,604 new coronavirus cases, according to a database maintained by The *Times*," the reporter wrote. "If the rates of contagiousness in Massachusetts and New York were to apply nationwide, then perhaps only 4,500 of those people may actually need to isolate and submit to contact tracing."[18]

Thus did we discover that perhaps 90% of the positive cases were not only asymptomatic, and not only non-contagious, but never should have been marked as positive in the first place. Maybe. To think that governors in the US had been using this case data the entire time to determine when and to what extent to permit openness. To top it off, the CDC in August announced that in only 6% of deaths attributed to Covid-19 was the virus listed as the sole cause.

Sometimes it appears that we know not much more today than we did even at the outset, simply because lockdowns have created such chaos and the trillions spent by governments on finding and killing Covid-19 have distorted information flows so seriously. How much clearer would matters be had we never taken this direction?

---

18 Mandavilli, Apoorva, "Your Coronavirus Test Is Positive. Maybe It Shouldn't Be." *New York Times*, August 29, 2020.

Smart Society, Stupid People

We've lived through the most bizarre experience of human folly in my lifetime, and perhaps in generations. Among the strangest aspects of it was the near universal failure on the part of regular people, and even the appointed "experts" (the ones the government employs, in any case), to have internalized anything about the basics of viruses that my mother understands, thanks to her mother before her who had a solid education in the subject after World War II.

Thus, for example, are all governments ready to impose new lockdowns should the infection data turn in the other direction? Under what theory, precisely, is this supposed to help matters? How does reimposing stay-home orders or mandating gym closures mysteriously manage to intimidate a virus into going away? "Run away and hide" seems to have replaced anything like a sophisticated understanding of viruses and immunities.

So I decided to download *Molecular and Cell Biology for Dummies* just to check if I was crazy.[19] I was pleased to see that it clearly stated that there are only two ways to defeat a virus: natural immunity and vaccines. The book completely left out the option that almost the entire world embraced in March: destroy businesses, force everyone to hide in their homes, and make sure that no one gets close to anyone else. The reason that the text leaves that out is that the idea is essentially ridiculous, so much so that it was initially sold as a strategy to preserve hospital space and only later mutated into a general principle that the way to beat a virus is to sanitize everything, avoid people and wear a mini-hazmat suit. Here is the passage:

---

19 Kratz, Rene Fester. 2009. *Molecular and Cell Biology For Dummies.* John Wiley & Sons.

For all of recorded history, humans have done a deadly dance with viruses. Measles, smallpox, polio, and influenza viruses changed the course of human history: Measles and smallpox killed hundreds of thousands of Native Americans; polio killed and crippled people, including US President Franklin Delano Roosevelt; and the 1918 influenza epidemic killed more people than were killed during all of World War I.

For most viruses that attack humans, your only defenses are prevention and your own immune systems. Antibiotics don't kill viruses, and scientists haven't discovered many effective antiviral drugs.

Vaccines are little pieces of bacteria or viruses injected into the body to give the immune system an education. They work by ramping up your own defensive system so that you're ready to fight the bacteria or virus upon first contact, without becoming sick first. However, for some viral diseases no vaccines exist, and the only option is to wait uncomfortably for your immune system to win the battle.

A virus is not a miasma, a cootie, or red goo like in the children's book *The Cat in the Hat*. There is no path toward waging, much less winning, a national war against a virus. It cares nothing about borders, executive orders, and titles. A virus is a thing to battle one immune system at a time, and our bodies have evolved to be suited to do just that. Vaccines can give advantage to the immune system through a clever hack. Even so, there will always be another virus and another battle, and so it's been for hundreds of thousands of years.

If you read the above carefully, you now know more than you would know from watching 50 TED talks on viruses by Bill Gates. Despite having thrown hundreds of millions of dollars into cobbling together some global plan to combat microbes, his own understanding seems not to have risen above a cooties theory of "run away and hide." There is another level of virus comprehension that came to be observed in the 1950s and then codified in the 1970s. For many viruses, not everyone has to catch them to become immune and not everyone needs a vaccine if there is one. Immunity is achieved when a certain percentage of the population has contracted some form of virus, with symptoms or without, and then the virus effectively dies.

This has important implications because it means that vulnerable demographics can isolate for the active days of the virus, and return to normal life once "herd immunity" has been realized with infection within some portion of the non-vulnerable population. This is why every bit of medical advice for elderly people has been to avoid large crowds during the flu season and why non-vulnerable groups getting and recovering from certain types of illnesses is a good thing.

What you get from this virus advice is not fear but calm management. This wisdom – not ignorance but wisdom – was behind the do-no-harm approach to the polio epidemic of 1949-1952, the Asian flu of 1957-58, and the Hong Kong flu of 1968-69. Donald Henderson summed up this old wisdom beautifully: "Communities faced with epidemics or other adverse events respond best and with the least anxiety when the normal social functioning of the community is least disrupted."

And that's what we did for the one hundred years following the cata-strophic Spanish flu of 1918. We never again attempted widespread closures or lockdown precisely because those policies had failed so miserably in the few places they were attempted. The cooties theory attempted a comeback with the Swine flu of 2009 (H1N1) but the world was too busy dealing with a financial crisis so the postwar strategy of virus control and mitigation prevailed once again, thankfully. But then the perfect storm hit in 2020 and a new generation of virus mitigators got their chance to conduct a grand social experiment based on computer modeling and forecasting.[20] Next thing you know, we had this new vocabulary shoved down our throats and we all had to obey strangely arbitrary exhortations.

"Go inside! No, wait, don't go inside!"
"Stay healthy but shut the gyms!"

---

20 Magness, Phillip W. 2020. "How Wrong Were the Models and Why?" *American Institute for Economic Research*, April 23.

"Get away from the virus but don't travel!"

"Don't wear a mask, wait, do wear a mask!"

"Only gather in groups if you are protesting Trump."

People started believing crazy things, as if we were medieval peasants, such as if there is a group of people or you stand too close to someone, the bad virus will spontaneously appear and you will get infected. Or that you could be a secret superspreader even if you have no symptoms, and also you can get the virus by touching almost anything. Good grief, the sheer amount of unscientific phony baloney unleashed in these terrible six months boggles the mind. But that's what happens in any panic. Apparently.

Now, something has truly been bugging me these months as I've watched the incredible unravelling of most of the freedoms we've long taken for granted. People were locked out of the churches and schools, businesses were shuttered, markets were closed, governors shoved through shelter-in-place orders meant not for disease control but aerial bomb raids, and masks were mandatory, all while regular people who otherwise seem smart hopped around each other like grasshoppers.

My major shock was discovering how much sheer stupidity exists in the population, particularly among the political class. Forgive a defense of my use of the term "stupid" but it is technically correct. I take it from Albert Camus and his brilliant book *The Plague*.[21] "When a war breaks out, people say: 'It's too stupid; it can't last long.' But though a war may well be 'too stupid,' that doesn't prevent its lasting. Stupidity has a knack of getting its way."

Indeed it is true. It was only last February when we seemed smart. We had amazing technology, movies on demand, a smartphone in our pockets to communicate with everyone and reveal all the world's knowledge. There was peace more or less. There was prosperity. There was progress. Our medical systems worked. It seemed that only a few months ago, we had it all together. We seemed smart. Until suddenly stupidity took over, or so it seemed.

---

21 Camus, Albert. 1947. *The Plague*. Random House Inc.: US.

Actually we weren't smart as individuals. Our politicians were as dumb as they ever have been, and massive ignorance pervaded the population, then as always. What was smart last February was society and the processes that made society work in the good old days.

"Please explain."

I shall.

Consider the social analytics of F.A. Hayek. His major theme is that the workings of the social order require knowledge and intelligence, but none of this essential knowledge subsists within any individual mind much less any political leader. The knowledge and intelligence necessary for society to thrive is instead decentralized throughout society, and comes to be embedded or instantiated within institutions and processes that gradually evolve from the free actions and choices of individuals.

What are those institutions? Market prices, supply chains, observations we make from the successful or unsuccessful choices of others that inform our habits and movements, manners and mores that work as social signals, interest rates that carefully coordinate the flow of money with our time preferences and risk tolerances, and even morals that govern our treatment of each other. All these come together to create a form of social intelligence that resides not in individual minds but rather the process of social evolution itself.

The trouble is that a well-functioning society can create an illusion that it all happens not because of the process but rather because we are so damn smart or maybe we have wise leaders with a good plan. It seems like it must be so, else how could we have become so good at what we do? Hayek's main point is that it is a mistake to credit individual intelligence or knowledge, much less good governments with brainy leaders, with civilizational achievements; rather, the real credit belongs to institutions and processes that no one in particular controls.

"To understand our civilisation," Hayek writes, "one must appreciate that the extended order resulted not from human design or intention but spontaneously: it arose from unintentionally conforming to certain traditional and largely moral practices, many of which men tend to dislike, whose significance they usually fail to understand, whose validity they cannot prove, and which have nonetheless fairly rapidly spread by means of an evolutionary selection — the comparative increase of population and wealth — of those groups that happened to follow them."

The lockdowns took a sledgehammer to these practices, processes, and institutions. It replaced them nearly overnight with new bureaucratic and police-state mandates that herded us into our homes and arbitrarily assigned new categories: elective vs. non-elective medical procedures, essential vs nonessential business, permissible vs. impermissible forms of association, even to the point of measuring the distance from which we must be separated one from another. And just like that, via executive order, many of the institutions and processes were crushed under the boot of the political class.

What emerged to take its place? It's sad to say but the answer is widespread ignorance. Despite having access to all the world's knowledge in our pockets, vast numbers of politicians and regular people defaulted back to a pre-modern cognition of disease. People did this out of fear, and were suddenly and strangely acquiescent to political commands. I've had friends tell me that they were guilty of this back in the day, believing that mass death was imminent so the only thing to do was to shelter in place and comply with the edicts.

The seeming intelligence that we had in February suddenly seemed to turn to mush. A better way to understand this is all our smartest institutions and practices were crushed, leaving only raw stupidity in its place. Truth is that we as individuals are probably not much smarter than our ancestors; the reason we've made so much progress is due to the increasing sophistication of Hayek's extended orders of association, signalling, capital accumulation, and technological know-how, none of which are due to wise leaders in government and industry but are rather attributable to the wisdom of the institutions we've gradually built over decades, centuries, and a millennia. Take those away and you reveal what we don't really want to see.

Looking back, I'm very impressed at the knowledge and awareness that the postwar generation had toward disease mitigation. It was taught in the schools, handed down several generations, and practiced in journalism and public affairs. That was smart. Something happened in the 21st century to cause a kind of breakage in that medical knowledge chain, and thus did societies around the world become vulnerable in the presence of a new virus: rule by charlatans, hucksters, media howlers, and would-be dictators.

With lockdown finally easing, we will see the return of what seems to be smart societies, and the gradual loss of the influence of Stupid. But let us not deceive ourselves. It could be that we've learned nothing from the fiasco that unfolded before our eyes. If economies come to be restored, eventually, to their former selves, it will not be because we (or our leaders) somehow beat a virus. The virus outsmarted everyone. What will fix what the political class has broken is the freedom once again to piece back together the institutions and processes that create the extended order that makes us all feel smarter than we really are.

.

Is Immunity a Case of Rothbard's
Lost Knowledge?

Murray Rothbard's wonderful *History of Economic Thought* opens with a blast against what he called the Whig theory of intellectual history.[22] It's a variant of the Victorian-era idea that life is always getting better and better, no matter what. Apply it to the world of ideas, and the impression is that our current ideas are always better than ideas of the past. It rules out the possibility that there is lost knowledge in history, peculiar incidences when humanity knew something for sure and then that knowledge mysteriously went away and we had to discover it again.

I'm writing this under a five-month near-global lockdown for fear of a new virus. A major epidemiologist in the UK, Raj S. Bhopal, dared to say precisely what my mother said at the outset of this disease: the way we must manage it is to develop natural immunities to it.[23] Yes, he said the taboo thing: people who face no fatal threat need to get it. This is precisely what my mother told me back in February.

It's a bit late but at least the subject is finally on the table. The idea of (badly named) herd immunity is consistent with how all societies have come to manage diseases.[24] Protect the vulnerable while groups at no or

---

22 Rothbard, Murray N. 2010. *"An Austrian Perspective on the History of Economic Thought."* *Mises Institute*, September 1.

23 Bhopal, Raj S. 2020. "COVID-19 zugzwang: Potential public health moves towards population (herd) immunity." *Public Health in Practice*, July 15.

24 Klein, Daniel B. 2020. "Herd Immunity Is Misleading." *American Institute for Economic Research*, May 11.

low risk acquire the immunities. It is especially important to understand this if you want to preserve freedom rather than vainly impose a police state out of fear and ignorance. It's extremely odd that we woke up one day in the 21st century when such knowledge seemed almost to evaporate. When famed statistician and immunologist Knut Wittkowski went public with the basics of viruses, he created shock and scandal.[25] YouTube even deleted his videos!

How did my mother know about immunities? Because her mother taught this to her, and hers before her. It was a major public-health priority after World War II in the United States to school each generation in this counterintuitive truth. It was taught in the schools: do not fear what we have evolved to fight but rather strengthen what nature has given you to deal with disease. Professor Bhopal dared say what few others have been willing to say but which seems obviously the case when you look at areas of the world where the effects of the virus are well- managed (New York and Sweden, for example).

My next question: why is herd immunity a taboo topic in the 21st century? Perhaps this is a case of Rothbardian-style lost knowledge, similar to how humanity once understood scurvy and then didn't and then had to come to understand it again.[26] Somehow in the 21st century, we find ourselves in the awkward position of having to relearn the basics of immunology that everyone from 1920 to 2000 or so seemed to understand before that knowledge somehow came to be marginalized and buried.

Yes, this is hugely embarrassing. The science never left the textbooks. It's right there for anyone to discover. What seems to have gone missing is popular understanding, replaced with a premodern run-and-hide theory of disease avoidance. It's so bad that even the imposition of police states around the country, including brutal shutdowns and house arrest, have not inspired anywhere near the level of public resistance that I would have expected. It's like everyone gradually became ignorant on the whole topic

---

25 Stringham, Edward Peter. 2020. "Stand Up for Your Rights, says Bio-Statistician Knut M. Wittkowski." *American Institute for Economic Research*, April 6.

26 Holding, Andrew N. 2010. "Forgotten Knowledge: The Science of Scurvy." *The Naked Scientists*, November 28.

and so they were caught off guard when politicians announced we had to get rid of human rights to fight a novel virus.

Here is Rothbard on this problem of lost knowledge and the Whig theory that such things do not happen:

> The **Whig theory**, subscribed to by almost all historians of science, including economics, **is that scientific thought progresses** patiently, one year after another developing, sifting, and testing theories, so **that science marches onward and upward, each year, decade or generation learning more and possessing ever more correct scientific theories.**
>
> On analogy with the Whig theory of history, coined in mid-nineteenth century England, which maintained that things are always getting (and therefore must get) better and better, the Whig historian of science, seemingly on firmer grounds than the regular Whig historian, implicitly or explicitly asserts that 'later is always better' in any particular scientific discipline.
>
> The Whig historian (whether of science or of history proper) really maintains that, for any point of historical time, 'whatever was, was right,' or at least better than 'whatever was earlier.' The inevitable result is a complacent and infuriating Panglossian optimism. In the historiography of economic thought, the consequence is the firm if implicit position that every individual economist, or at least every school of economists, contributed their important mite to the inexorable upward march. There can, then, be no such thing as gross systemic error that deeply flawed, or even invalidated, an entire school of economic thought, much less sent the world of economics permanently astray.

Rothbard's entire book is an exercise in discovering lost knowledge. He was fascinated with how A.R.J. Turgot could have written with such clarity about value theory but the later writings of Adam Smith were murky on the topic. He was intrigued that the classical economists were lucid on the status of economic theory but later economists in the 20th century became so confused about it. You could observe the same about free trade doctrine: once it was understood almost universally such that everyone seemed to agree it had to be a priority to build peace and prosperity, and then — poof! — that knowledge seems to have vanished in recent years.

On a personal note, I recall how passionate Murray felt about the issue of lost knowledge. He was also urging his students to find cases, document them, and explain how it happens. He always suspected that there were more cases that needed to be discovered and investigated. His writings on the history of ideas are a major effort to document as many cases as he could find.

Another intriguing feature: one might suppose that knowledge would be less likely to be lost in the information age in which we all carry in our pockets access to nearly all the world's information. We can access it with just a few clicks. How did this not protect us against falling prey to a medieval-style theory of disease management? How did our fears and reliance of computer modeling so easily displace inherited wisdom of the past? Why did this new virus trigger brutal attacks on rights whereas nothing like this has happened in the previous century of new viruses?

George Washington's troops scraped off the scabs of the smallpox dead to inoculate themselves, but we cower in our homes in fear and obedience for a virus that is 99.6% non-fatal and is fatal mostly for people who lived four years longer than the average life span.[27] Friends of mine who caught the virus and developed immunities are still treated like lepers even though there is not one single verified case of reinfection from Covid-19 in the world.

I can only say this. Murray Rothbard right now would be astonished at how medical ignorance, fake science, and the lust for power all combined so suddenly to create the greatest global crisis in modern history for the cause of liberty to which he devoted his life. If anything has demonstrated that Rothbard was correct about the fallacy of the Whig theory, and the capacity of humanity suddenly to act in total ignorance of what was once widely known, it is these last six months of folly.

---

27 Tucker, Jeffrey A. 2020. "The American Revolution Occurred in the Middle of a Pandemic." *American Institute for Economic Research*, July 4.

The Virus Doesn't Care
About Your Policies

Based on the data, there seems to be no relationship between lockdowns and lives saved. That's remarkable, given that we know for sure that lockdowns have destroyed economies the world over.

Every epidemic model being flung around in March was built with the assumption that lockdowns would control the virus. In the early days, it was about preserving hospital capacity. Later it became a general principle: slow the spread. The methods were the same in nearly every country. Ban large gatherings. Close schools. Shutter businesses. Enforce stay-at-home orders. Mandate human separation. Masks. Travel restrictions.

Nothing like this had been tried in the whole history of humanity, certainly not on this scale. You might suppose, then, there was absolute certainty that there would be a causal relationship between lockdowns and the trajectory of the virus. Just as the FDA doesn't approve a drug unless it is proven to be safe and effective, one might suppose the same would be true for a policy that shattered every routine and trampled human rights in the name of disease mitigation. Surely!

It turns out that this was not the case. It was pure speculation that lockdowns would suppress this virus, and that speculation was based on a hubristic presumption of the awesome power and intelligence of government managers. For six months, governments all over the world have been freaking out, ordering people around to do this and that, passing mandate after mandate, and yet there is no evidence that any of it matters to the virus.

Already in mid-April questions arose. Prof Isaac Ben-Israel, head of the Security Studies program at Tel Aviv University and the chairman of the National Council for Research and Development, looked at the data around the world and concluded that the virus comes and goes after 70 days regardless of the policies deployed.[28] He found no relationship at all between locking down and transmission or death.

Fast forward to mid-July. Data scientists investigated the experience from the spring.[29] They too found no relationship between the virus and policy. Putting it very bluntly: "Rapid border closures, full lockdowns, and wide-spread testing were not associated with Covid-19 mortality per million people." That's awesome to consider. Billions of lives fundamentally altered. Economies wrecked. Centuries-old traditions of liberty and law thrown out. Police-states everywhere. And to what end? The data indicate it was all for naught. Apparently, you cannot control a virus with state policies. The virus just doesn't seem to care.

One helpful tool you can use to observe this comes from a website called "Our World in Data," which offers a stringency index of government policies based on data from Oxford University.[30] Look at the index based on the countries in the world with the highest Covid-19 mortality rates. They are San Marino, Belgium, UK, Spain, Peru, Italy, Chile, USA, France, Brazil, Netherlands, and Mexico.

Most of these governments imposed a quick lockdown at about the same time, followed by a gradual and scattered effort to liberalize. Sweden is the great outlier here, of course. They all had high mortality rates, with some higher and some lower than Sweden. Counterfactuals are impossible, of course, but already this chart raises questions about whether and to what extent policies had anything at all to do with preventing deaths.

Another way to look at this is to compare the top six countries with the highest mortality per millions with the six significant countries with

---

28 Wikipedia. 2020. "Isaac Ben-Israel." *Wikipedia*, July 7; Times of Israel Staff. 2020. "Top Israeli prof claims simple stats show virus plays itself out after 70 days." *Times of Israel*, April 19.

29 Chaudhry, Rabail, George Dranitsaris, Talha Mubashir, Justyna Bartoszko, and Sheila Riazi. 2020. "A country level analysis measuring the impact of government actions, country preparedness and socioeconomic factors on COVID-19 mortality and related health outcomes." *The Lancet*, 100464.

30 Our World in Data. 2020. "COVID-19: Government Response Stringency Index." *OurWorldinData.org*.

the lowest mortality per million. Those low-mortality countries are: Uganda, Burundi, Mozambique, Tanzania, Rwanda and Sri Lanka. All these countries locked down. There is no relationship between death and locking down vs. staying open. Consider 12 countries with very similar deaths per million (50, plus or minus 10). You can observe a huge range of policies, and no apparent relationship between those policies and outcomes in terms of deaths.

Here is a global chart of deaths per million compared with lockdown severity. You can look at it all day but it shows absolutely nothing meaningful in terms of policy.[31]

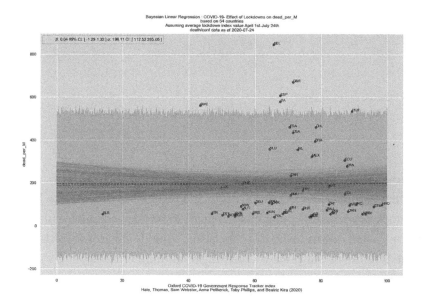

Plotting only European countries yields a slightly strange result, a pattern but the opposite of what we are supposed to see. Todd Kenyon used the Oxford data to show that the tighter the lockdown, the higher the deaths per million. There might be many other explanations for this but, here again, we see nothing suggesting that lockdowns improved outcomes.

––––––––––––––

31 tolex 3. 2020. "Bayesian Linear Regression: COVID-19 Effect of Lockdowns on dead_per_M." *GitHub*, July 24.

In "Did Lockdown Work? An Economist's Cross-Country Comparison" Christian Bjørnskov finds "no clear association between lockdown policies and mortality development," while offering the following chart:[32]

Figure 1. Mortality development in 2020, two groups

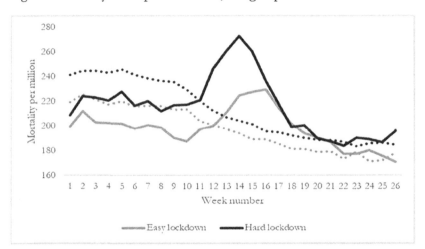

You can do the comparison within the United States, thanks to this excellent study by five economists.[33] The results are the same: whether you lock down or stay open there appears to be no predictable pattern in deaths. If lockdowns saved lives, the curve should slant downwards to the right. It doesn't slant at all. It's seemingly random. Once again, it's almost as if the virus doesn't care.

Now, you could take apart this data on grounds that it is too aggregated, that there are too many variables based on demographics (average age of death across the world is 82 with comorbidities, nearly half in nursing homes), and so on. But at some point, we are going to have to throw in the towel. Whether a country locked down or stayed open has as much

32 Bjørnskov, Christian. 2020. "Did Lockdown Work? An Economist's Cross-Country Comparison." *SSRN*, August 2.

33 McCann, Adam. 2020. "States with the Fewest Coronavirus Restrictions." *WalletHub*, August 11.

predictive power over deaths per million as whether it rains today is related to the color of my socks. Or whether hurricanes are controlled by literacy rates. In other words, the claim that "lockdowns control viruses" is pseudoscience or magical thinking of a deeply dangerous sort; it wrecks economies and lives.

To be sure, there are plenty of studies claiming that lockdowns saved lives but the high-profile ones are model-based extrapolations that presume the existence of a relationship that the facts do not seem to back up. If there is a broad-based research study using real data that demonstrates something life-saving about destroying rights and liberties in the name of virus control, I've yet to see it. Meanwhile, a National Bureau of Economic Research (NBER) working paper by Andrew Atkeson, Karen Kopecky, and Tao Zha focused on countries and US states with more than 1,000 Covid-19 deaths as of late July. In all, the study included 25 US states and 23 countries. As Stephen Miller writes, "The paper's conclusion is that the data trends observed above likely indicate that nonpharmaceutical interventions (NPIs) – such as lockdowns, closures, travel restrictions, stay-home orders, event bans, quarantines, curfews, and mask mandates – do not seem to affect virus transmission rates overall."[34]

Meanwhile, we are overwhelmed with evidence that it was all pointlessly destructive. Liberty means the practice of health and wealth; lockdowns lead to exactly what D.A. Henderson predicted: catastrophe.

---

34 Miller, Stephen. 2020. "Lockdowns and Mask Mandates Do Not Lead to Reduced COVID Transmission Rates or Deaths, New Study Suggests," *American Institute for Economic Research*, August 26.

The Bloodless Political Class
and Its Lack of Empathy

Why watch Covid-19 press conferences and briefings by politicians? They are just upsetting. These people seem to have no clue about why the virus is ignoring them. They keep issuing strange and arbitrary rules that they make up, change by the day, all enforced by intimidation and compulsion. They posture in this silly way as if their edicts have this virus under control when they clearly do not.

Even worse, and what has chilled me to the bone, is the strange absence of normal human emotion in their public performances. With day-to-day human communication in the presence of uncertainty, you would think there would be some admission of the possibility of being wrong, of mistakes made, of the difficulty of knowing, of the limits of information to make informed decisions, of the pain wrought through such disruptive governance.

You don't see any of this in these governor's announcements.[35] Despite all evidence, they act as if they have got this under control. They don't admit error. They don't admit ignorance. They stare straight at the cameras and issue edicts, without even an apology for all the lives they have ruined and continue to ruin. They talk down to us. Condescension in every word.

We don't talk this way to each other. Instead we share stories of how our lives have been affected. We share pain with each other, and frustration at how destabilized we feel, how we've been separated from family, how lockdowns have led us to dark places, how caged we feel. We worry about our finances, our loved ones, our very futures. We are astonished at

---

35 MassGovernor. 2020. "COVID-19 Update: New Travel Order Effective August 1st." *YouTube*, July 24.

how quickly and radically our freedoms were taken away. And in sharing these stories with each other, we come to understand more and feel a bit of healing perhaps.

In short, we have empathy. The politicians on the other hand have shown none. They have glassy eyes that reflect cold blood. Even worse, they come across as heartless, like generals who order troops around knowing with certainty that many people will die. They rarely, if ever, talk about what they are doing in human terms. They talk about data, restrictions, trends in infections and hospitalizations, and death, but not as if any of this involves real people or tradeoffs. They preen with certainly that is not really believable.

Adam Smith explained empathy as a feature of the human personality. "As we have no immediate experience of what other men feel," he wrote, "we can form no idea of the manner in which they are affected, but by conceiving what we ourselves should feel like in the situation […] By the imagination we place ourselves in his situation, we conceive ourselves enduring all the same torments […] and become in some measure the same person with him."

That's what real life is like. But political life today seems to seek to banish that very human feeling. It's as if they are playing a video game featuring all of us but we are mere figures on a screen programmed to do what they want. They have no obligation to understand us, much less worry about the pain they inflict, because, like figures on a gaming screen, we surely don't feel pain at all. And that is also how the media has come to talk of this calamity. Its numbers, charts, and trends, all highly alarmist and always with the same conclusion: the political class needs to impose more restrictions on us to make this virus go away. We sit helpless watching all of this unfold day after day, astonished that our rules could be so impervious to what has taken place before our eyes.

The emotional gap between the rulers and ruled has never been wider in modern times. It seems completely unsustainable. It's like they aren't even trying to connect with people. Politicians are no great shakes in normal times but they seem worse than ever now, throwing out law, tradition, morality, and even the appearance of caring about how their lockdowns have destroyed so many lives. The question is why. Here is my attempt at an answer. The lockdowns have all been based on an implausible claim that viruses can be controlled via coercion, same as people can be. But they cannot. And it is not surprising to find enormous evidence, accumulating by the day, that everything they have done has achieved nothing.

Compare Covid-19 deaths per million around the world against Oxford University's government stringency index.[36] If lockdowns achieved anything you could expect there to be some predictive power here. The more you lock down, the more lives you save. The lockdown countries could at least claim to have bolstered the lives of their citizens. What you see instead is: nothing. There is no relationship. There is the virus. There are lockdowns. The two operate as seemingly independent variables.

The political class has started to intuit this. They suspect in their heart of hearts that they have done something horrendous. They worry that this realization is going to spread. Then they will be held accountable, maybe not right away but eventually. And this is rather terrifying to them. Thus are they spending their days trying to forestall this moment of truth in hopes that the mess they made will eventually go away and they escape blame.

Which is to say: they are lying. Then they lie more to cover their previous lies. If you are going to push such a line in the face of the mounting evidence showing them to be frauds, if you are going to lie with impunity to keep the game going, you will have to steel yourself against emotion and empathy. You become a sociopath. This might be enough to account for their bloodless posturing.

There is another factor too: the more pain you inflict on people, the worse of a person you become. Power is dangerous even when not used, but deploying it brutally and pointlessly rots the soul. This is a good description of almost the entire ruling class around the world today, save a few civilized countries that never locked down.

---

36 tolex3. 2020. "lockdown_index_dead_per_M.jpg." *GitHub*, July 27.

The Return of Brutalism

The lockdowners probably had no idea what they were about to unleash. On paper, their plans all seemed fine. Keep people apart. Make them stay home. Only essential workers should go to work. Government can do the rest. Church, theaters, sports, bars, schools – everything has to give way to rule by disease mitigators.

Let the kids play computer games. Let the offices operate through Zoom. A bit of time off never hurt anyone, and, besides, there is Netflix. We'll beat this virus by hiding from it, and then it'll get bored and go back where it came from. The model builders will be heroes. We only need to demonstrate the power of computers over even the awesome and previously uncontrollable forces of nature. The virus will relent in the face of our intelligence, power, and resources.

What they did not expect were riots in the streets, toppled statues, secession movements, the rise of political extremism on all sides, the fueling of racial conflict, and the spread of nihilism. What's happening all over the world feels like revolution. Once you lock down a population by executive fiat, based on obvious ignorance and fear, you send a signal that nothing much matters anymore. Nothing is true, permanent, right, wrong. Might as well tear it all down. You literally unleash Hell.

There is plenty of historical precedent for this but one episode has long intrigued me. It concerns the rise of Brutalist architecture after World War II. The movement was about stripping adornments from buildings, forgetting about beauty, eschewing aesthetics of the past, and designing for temporality and functionality only.

Brutalism, which began in Germany as a successor to the Bauhaus movement following the Great War, is the movement that eventually gave us all the ghastly government buildings in the US that were put up in the 1960s through to the 1990s. They are concrete, sparse, and just slightly horrible to the eye because they are meant to be. It was a movement that rejected aesthetics. It wanted and demanded the raw truth: a building is to be occupied. It should only be "essential" and nothing more.

After World War II, the question concerned what should replace that which was bombed and destroyed in wartime, the worst example of which was Dresden, which faced unbelievable destruction. Eventually that city and all its glorious architecture was restored. But the shock that governments could just smash everything in sight, that nothing was sacred, was a lesson that impacted a whole generation of designers. Throughout the rest of Germany and most of the rest of Europe, the UK, and the US, the lesson was: buildings should be bombable. That way, nothing of value is lost.

That is the spirit that drove the Brutalist school to be so influential. Many old buildings, from the Middle Ages through the early 20th century, were constructed with high aspirations, including theological ones. But the war demonstrated that everything is temporary. Nothing is really true or sacred. God is dead else countless millions would not have been slaughtered. Our postwar architecture should embrace the reality that we learned in wartime, which is that nothing much matters in the end. Everything can be bombed. Nothing is beyond destruction. Hence the past should die and everything new should be expendable.

This is nihilism. It is an expression of despair. It is a cry against the idea that the future and past should have any relationship to each other. Might as well tear down the monuments. Burn buildings. Have riots in the streets. And while we're at it, let's forget logic, rationality, the lessons of history, and even humane concern for others. Our governments, democratically elected, clearly care nothing for the rule of law, empathy, morality, and lack all humility, so why should we not believe the same things and behave the same way?

The rage that pent up between March 15 and June 1, 2020 expressed itself in many ways. You know this from your own life. Think of the relationships that were shattered, how you took out your anger on those you love, and they on you, and how you said and did things that would have been unthinkable this time last year. The lockdowns made everyone a bit pathological. I'm not talking only about the spike in suicides and drug overdoses. I'm speaking of the casual cruelty that people dabbled in over these months, the way in which our old codes of manners, discipline, character, and integrity suddenly seemed irrelevant. Truth and lies blended in a confusing mush.

After all, if governments can really lock us in our homes, slice and dice the population into essential and nonessential, close our houses of worship, force us to mask our faces, and demand that we hop around like grasshoppers to avoid each other, what does that say about the codes of morality and human decency we've built up over generations? If governments don't care, why should we? To some extent or another, everyone has dabbled in this form of nihilism over the last 75 days. For many people, this has tumbled into destructionism itself.[37]

In the best of worlds, what is true and right should not hinge on government's treatment of essential rights. In reality, it makes a huge difference. If governments care nothing for our freedom of movement and our economic rights, why should anyone really? This is the essence of the Brutalist view of life. Just get it done. We only need essentials. Everything else is expendable. Nothing else matters, not context, truth, decency, the past, or the future.

You could say to me that the riots and destruction and the sheer insanity all around us are not obviously connected to lockdown. I disagree. The protestors, rioters, statue topplers, and building burners might not articulate the precise reasons for their behavior. But if you look carefully, what you see is people crying out with a demand that governments and establishments pay attention to what the people want. People matter. Volition matters. We cannot be locked down. We are not animals and nor will we be treated as automatons in agent-based models. We won't be part of someone else's idea of history. We are history.

In this way, governments have pushed us all into adopting a Brutalist theory of life, if only because they made the first move and now we have no choice but to fight back. Brutality will be met with brutality. To be sure, I'm not endorsing this view of the world. I find it highly regrettable

---

37 Tucker, Jeffrey A. 2019. "The Joker and the Ideology of Destructionism." *American Institute for Economic Research*, October 7.

and even immoral. It creates nothing. Still, when governments behave this way, as if freedom doesn't matter, this is what they unleash. They punish and drive out decency, integrity, and virtue. When you do that, you release unpredictable forces within society that make the world ugly, even terrifying.

There is an answer to this rampant incivility. Don't let governments and their egregious mismanagement of this crisis wreck your integrity, your capacity for love, your belief in rights, your aspirations for yourself and others. The only way to fight back against Brutalism is with freedom and beauty, and that begins in your own life.

When Will the Madness End?

I was sitting in the green room in a Manhattan television studio on the day that the storm seemed to hit. It was Thursday, March 12, 2020, and I was waiting anxiously for a TV appearance, hoping that the trains wouldn't shut down before I could leave the city. The trains never did shut but half of everything else did. On this day, everyone knew what was coming. There was disease panic in the air, fomented mostly by the media and political figures. A month earlier, the idea of lockdown was unthinkable, but now it seemed like it could happen, at any moment.

A thin, wise-looking bearded man with Freud-style glasses sat down across from me, having just left the studio. He was there to catch his breath following his interview but he looked deeply troubled.

"There is fear in the air," I said, breaking the silence.

"Madness is all around us. The public is adopting a personality disorder I've been treating my whole career."

"What is it that you do?" I asked.

"I'm a practicing psychiatrist who specializes in anxiety disorders, paranoid delusions, and irrational fear. I've been treating this in individuals as a specialist. It's hard enough to contain these problems in normal times. What's happening now is a spread of this serious medical condition to the whole population. It can happen with anything but here we see a primal fear of disease turning into mass panic. It seems almost deliberate. It is tragic. Once this starts, it could take years to repair the psychological damage."

I sat there a bit stunned, partially because speaking in such apocalyptic terms was new in those days, and because of the certitude of his opinion. Underlying his brief comments were a presumption that there was nothing particularly unusual about this virus. We've evolved with them, and learned to treat them with calm and professionalism. What distinguished the current moment, he was suggesting, was not the virus but the unleashing of a kind of public madness.

I was an early skeptic of the we-are-all-going-to-die narrative. But even I was unsure if he was correct that the real problem was not physical but mental. In those days, even I was cautious about shaking hands and carrying around sanitizer. I learned later, of course, that plenty of medical professionals had been trying to calm people down for weeks, urging the normal functioning of society rather than panic. It took weeks however even for me to realize that he was right: the main threat society faced was a psychological condition.

I should have immediately turned to a book that captivated me in high school. It is *Extraordinary Popular Delusions and the Madness of Crowds* by Charles Mackay.[38] I liked reading it because, while it highlighted human folly, it also seemed to indicate that we as a civilization are over that period in history. It allowed me to laugh at how ridiculous people were in the past, with sudden panics over long hair and beards, jewelry, witches, the devil, prophecies and sorcery, disease and cures, land speculation, tulips, just about anything. In a surprising number of cases he details, disease plays a role, usually as evidence of a malicious force operating in the world. Once fear reaches a certain threshold, normalcy, rationality, morality, and decency fade and are replaced by shocking stupidity and cruelty. He writes:

> In reading the history of nations, we find that, like individuals, they have their whims and their peculiarities; their seasons of excitement and recklessness, when they care not what they do. We find that whole communities suddenly fix their minds upon one object, and go mad in its pursuit; that millions of people become simultaneously impressed with one delusion, and run after it, till their attention is caught by some new folly more captivating than the first. We see one nation suddenly seized, from its highest to its lowest members, with a fierce desire of

---

38 Mackay, Charles. 1841. *Extraordinary Popular Delusions And The Madness Of Crowds.* Richard Bentley Publishers: London, UK.

military glory; another as suddenly becoming crazed upon a religious scruple; and neither of them recovering its senses until it has shed rivers of blood and sowed a harvest of groans and tears, to be reaped by its posterity. […] Men, it has been well said, think in herds; it will be seen that they go mad in herds, while they only recover their senses slowly, and one by one.

After 2005 when the Internet developed into a serious repository for human knowledge, and it became accessible via smartphones and near-universal access, I too was tempted by the idea that we would enter into a new age of enlightenment in which mass frenzies would be quickly stopped by dawning wisdom.

You can see evidence of my naiveté with my article on April 5, 2020: "With Knowledge Comes Calm, Rationality, and, Possibly, Openness."[39] My thought then was that the evidence of the extremely discriminatory impact of the virus on plus-70 people with underlying conditions would cause a sudden realization that this virus was behaving like a normal virus. We were not all going to die. We would use rationality and reopen. I recall writing that with a sense of confidence that the media would report the new study and the panic would end.

I was preposterously wrong, along with my four-month-old feeling that all of this stuff would stop on Monday. The psychiatrist I met in New York was correct: the drug of fear had already invaded the public mind. Once there, it takes a very long time to recover. This was made far worse by politics, which had only fed the beast of fear. This quickly became the most politicized disease in history, and as a consequence the political beast has done nothing to help manage it and much to make it all vastly worse.

We've learned throughout this ordeal that despite our technology, our knowledge, our history of building prosperity and peace, we are no smarter than our ancestors and, by some measures, not as smart as our parents and grandparents. The experience with Covid-19 has caused a mass reversion to the superstitions and panics that sporadically defined

---

39 Tucker, Jeffrey A. 2020. "With Knowledge Comes Calm, Rationality, and, Possibly, Openness." *American Institute for Economic Research*, April 5.

the human experience of ages past.

Eventually, people have and do come to their senses, but it is as Mackay said: people "go mad in herds, while they only recover their senses slowly, and one by one."

The Carnage

Why Did They Close the Schools?

On March 12, 2020, a banshee-like cry went out to an email list of public health professionals and government officials who were then in a state of mental meltdown. Pull the trigger now, screamed the memo. Close the schools.

As with any email chain, there were a few dominant voices who post more than others and with more passion, while others shrink back in fear of being shamed. Such was the case here: one disciple of computer modeling, Dr. Carter Mecher of the Veterans Administration, was convinced that the coronavirus was another Spanish Flu. Why? He didn't explain. Mostly he wanted to try out his closure/lockdown/social-distance model on which he had been working for 14 years since he first became a convert to agent-based modeling techniques. The Coronavirus of 2020 was as good an excuse as any.

Mecher emerged as the leader of the list, sending hundreds of messages of increasing alarm. Others had already joined in the alarm party. The *New York Times*'s Daniel McNeil had two weeks earlier publicly predicted as many as 6.6 million Americans would die. That is, if you had 300 friends, 6 of your friends would die from Covid-19.[40] He knew this because this virus "reminded" him of the Spanish Flu too.

Mecher, a longtime pusher of the cooties theory of viruses (in which running and hiding is always the answer), called for an immediate nationwide school closing, even though it was already apparent that Covid-19 represented almost zero threat to school kids. Pull the trigger

---

40 Tucker, Jeffrey A. 2020. "Why Does the New York Times Deny the Obvious?" *American Institute for Economic Research*, June 5.

now, he demanded. Do it all at once, now, attaching his long document filled with startling pictures of mass death and how school closures would stop that. It's no big deal, he promised. Kids love being home. It will bring families together (so long as they stay six feet apart).

Within days it happened. Then the dominos began to fall. If kids are home, parents have to be also. Offices and stores should close too. If they are older kids, they will congregate in malls and parks, so they must close too. So too amusement parks, bowling alleys, aquariums, museums, and anything but the most essential businesses.

In the blink of an eye, a nation locked down. Let us remember that it began domestically (Trump had already nonsensically banned international travel) with the schools, schools on which kids depend for education and social connection and parents pay for in taxes and tuition. States, without warning and with only evidence of crazed and fearful frenzy, shut their doors, thus sending tens of millions home and disrupting the lives of every American household.

On May 1, 2020, the prestige journal *The Lancet* said the following:[41]

> Currently, the evidence to support national closure of schools to combat COVID-19 is very weak and data from influenza outbreaks suggest that school closures could have relatively small effects on a virus with COVID-19's high transmissibility and apparent low clinical effect on school children. At the same time, these data also show that school closures can have profound economic and social consequences.

Whoops. So far as I know, Carter Mecher has had nothing to say these days.

---

41 Viner, Russell M., Simon J. Russell, Helen Croker, Jessica Packer, Joseph Ward, et al. 2020. "School closure and management practices during coronavirus outbreaks including COVID-19: a rapid systematic review." *The Lancet* 4(5): 397-404.

The Lockdowns Killed the Arts

What's closed in the arts? Nearly everything. Unless you want to switch on your laptop. Otherwise forget it. Hardly anyone is being paid for live performance of anything. Many volunteer choirs are banned from rehearsing. No, a fundamentalist totalitarian cult has not taken over. Something else has happened. Let's look at the carnage, starting with my memories of the dawn of this disaster.

The two people sitting next to me in the bar at the train station were despondent. They worked on Broadway. One was an instrumental musician and the other a singer. They had just received word that Broadway was shutting down – forced closed by the governor. This was the afternoon of March 12, 2020. Surely, they said, this would only be for a week or two, and I agreed. After all, this is Broadway! We toasted to a quick reopening. At the time of writing this (July 14, 2020), that was 123 days ago. On June 29, 2020, it had become official.[42] Broadway will remain closed for the rest of the year. The reopening date would later be changed to early 2021.

I have no idea what these nice people have done with their lives since then. Live music performances have been devastated by the lockdowns. Most of these artists live financially leveraged lives as it is, working and getting paid gig to gig. It's their one great skill. Vast numbers of them have been forcibly unemployed. I think of the pianist who plays at the local hotel lobby with a friend of his friends, the guitar band with a nightly gig at the pub, the choir conductor forced to sit on his hands for months, the band director who has no band, the movie director who sits on piles of

---

42 McPhee, Ryan. 2020. "Broadway Will Officially Remain Closed Through 2020." *Playbill*, June 29.

promising scripts, the struggling painter who can't display her art, the dancer with no opportunities for performance, the opera singer who faces 9 months of cancelled performances.

All of this in the name of disease management. Governments declared arts to be nonessential, dispensable, abolishable. It's the biggest attack on art and beauty possibly since the iconoclasm of the 16th century, when mobs sacked churches, tore out paintings, and melted candlesticks in bonfires. Back then the motivation was to purify the world of sin. Now we think we are purifying the world of disease.

Here in the Berkshires of Western Massachusetts, a regional tradition is the Tanglewood Music Festival. It's the summer home for the Boston Symphony Orchestra. All seasons, there are symphonies and chamber concerts, attracting tens of thousands of people who sit on the lawn or indoors, and attend lectures. In times when classical music is suffering, Tanglewood figured out how to make it fashionable and even profitable.

This year it was cancelled. The years of preparation, the contracts, the recordings, the logistics, the training camps, the professionals and professors – it was all taken away by government edict. The beautiful grounds are empty. It's not only an economic calamity. It's also a tragedy for civilization. And there's more:

- New York Ballet: cancelled.[43]
- Carnegie Hall and the Lincoln Center: closed for the rest of the year.[44]
- Kennedy Center: shut down.[45]
- Chicago Symphony: cancelled.[46]

---

43 Gans, Andrew. 2020. "New York City Ballet Cancels 2020 Fall Season." *Playball*, June 18.

44 Bahr, Sarah. 2020. "Carnegie Hall and Lincoln Center Cancel Fall Performances." *The New York Times*, June 18.

45 The Kennedy Center. 2020. "Kennedy Center Cancels Most Previously Scheduled Performances Through the End of 2020 Due to COVID-19." *The Kennedy Center*, June 23.

46 Frost, Crystal A. 2020. "'Nothing Like This Has Ever Happened': How Orchestra Musicians Are Faring In The Pandemic." *Grammy Awards*, June 17.

- Mormon Tabernacle Choir tour: cancelled.[47]
- Art Galleries all over the country: closed by force or economic necessity.[48]
- Chicago's theater events: a long list of devastation.[49]
- Church choirs all over the world: silenced.[50]
- The legendary Blue Note jazz club: shuttered until further notice.
- A choir in Texas was excoriated in the press for "singing without masks" when the VP visited.[51]

In the UK, the government has announced emergency funding for the arts including choirs to help with the pain. But as 200 leading musicians wrote in The *Telegraph*, they would far rather just get back to rehearsing and performing.[52] A tradition of composition and performance that dates back 500 years, along with cathedrals and choir schools and performance halls, has been treated savagely by the government, as if none of this really matters. Worse, these bureaucrats imagine that excellence in musical performance and teaching can be turned off and on like some kind of home appliance.

Consider, for example, the fate of children's choirs. Director Charles Cole writes:[53]

---

47 Walch, Tad. 2020. "Tabernacle Choir at Temple Square's summer tour postponed until 2021." *Deseret News*, April 27.

48 Schultz, Abby. 2020. "Art Galleries Report Steep Revenue Drops Amid Closures." *Barrons*, May 20.

49 Theatre in Chicago. 2020. "List of Chicago Theatre Events Canceled/Postponed Due to Coronavirus." *Theatre in Chicago.*

50 Kramer, Anna. 2020. "No singing, no chanting: Conservatives object to California's worship restrictions." *San Francisco Chronicle*, July 7.

51 Folley, Aris. 2020. "Choir of more than 100 people sings without masks at Pence event in Texas." *The Hill*, June 28.

52 Swerling, Gabriella. 2020. "Exclusive: Religious music 'under threat' warn composers and musicians." *The Telegraph*, July 10.

53 Cole, Charles. 2020. "Choirs: An Appeal for Common Sense." *New Liturgical Movement*, June 28.

Children's choirs are in a constant state of flux and development and boys' voices undergo pronounced change which requires particular management. Throughout a choir, individuals are at different stages of sight-reading proficiency, pitching ability and general musical awareness. The younger ones apprentice from the older ones, with every child at a different stage on the journey. Through this process the transmission of the choral tradition itself takes place, encompassing the shared musical experiences, the collegiate knowledge of specific repertoire, and the choir's unique sound itself, melded by the building in which it sings.

None of this can be simply put on hold; it has to be active in order to exist. This is certainly the case for the two choirs which I direct, the London Oratory Junior Choir and the London Oratory Schola, on whose behalf I wrote to Oliver Dowden MP, the Secretary of State for Digital, Culture, Media and Sport to express these concerns.

Cole only received a form letter back.

As a one-time choral conductor myself, I know how difficult it is to restart after just a few weeks off. But four months during prime performance season? It's brutal and ignorant. How many years will it take to repair this damage? How many institutions are going to go belly up? Imagine England without Handel's Messiah, William Byrd or Thomas Tallis, or even the hymns of Ralph Vaughan Williams! Why would people have done this to our precious arts communities, and why are so few objecting or even talking about it? For that matter, what is America without live jazz, Broadway, and the movies in theaters? What the hell is going on here?

The excuse is disease control, as if choirs and jazz clubs are nothing but germ spreading machines. There is no particular reason to believe it, given the wild exaggerations of the threat out there for a virus that reached its national fatality peak six months ago.

I will provide an empirical case from three weeks ago when I was among 400 plus people gathered from all over the country in a New Hampshire campground for PorcFest.[54] There was no distancing and almost no mask wearing. You might think it would become a Covid-19 petri dish based on the frenzy alive in the media. Actually a survey following the 3-day event turned up not one single case of sickness. Not one!

Based on this and piles of evidence mounting daily that the fatalities of this disease are predictably focused on the very old and sick, it seems hopelessly ignorant to have done this to the arts community.

A civilization without art is not a high civilization. Maybe it doesn't even deserve the name.

Sometimes people use the word philistine to refer to someone who doesn't appreciate art. If that's true, what word can we use for those who abolish the arts by force?

---

54 Tucker, Jeffrey A. 2020. "Broadway Closed but Porcfest Stayed Open." *American Institute for Economic Research*, June 29.

Porcfest Stayed Open

I t was the 17th year for the Porcupine Freedom Festival in Lancaster, New Hampshire, held at the Rogers Campground.[55] It was an unusually spirited, emotional, and powerful gathering this time, mostly because it took place in defiance of the fear-based culture that politicians and the media have been spreading for months. Hey, if Woodstock could take place during the Hong Kong Flu (which killed 100,000 Americans over the season), surely Porcfest should go ahead in the midst of whatever Covid-19 was.[56]

Because of the lockdowns and mandatory closures, desolation and despair has swept through many areas of the country, with boarded up businesses, plexiglass separating people, and sadness all around.[57] But here, for three days, all 400 or so of us got to experience something like what we might call the old world (meaning February and before): just happy people sharing ideas, eating, meeting, and enjoying themselves.

I'm sure that the organizers faced some pressure to call it off, but Carla Gericke looked past the propaganda and went ahead anyway. This year too was a bit different from usual, lacking some of the glitz and organizational formalism of the past. But we were no worse for it. There were talks on every aspect of health, economics, history, philosophy, commerce, crypto, firearms, Covid-19, and you name it. The main pavilion had something go

---

55 Porcfest. 2020. *Porcupine Freedom Festival.*

56 Tucker, Jeffrey A. 2020. "Woodstock Occurred in the Middle of a Pandemic." *American Institute for Economic Research*, May 1.

57 Gill, Anthony. 2020. "Tear Down this Plexiglass!" *American Institute for Economic Research*, June 17.

on day and night, and there were mini gatherings all over the campground.

Most people camp but there are also cabins and hotels for people like me. Even then, there is no getting around the "roughing it" aspect of the conference. You don't know when or where your next meal is coming from: that entirely depends on what food trucks happen to be there. Everything is on a "bring your own" basis. The view of the mountains from the campsite are remarkable and strangely therapeutic.

In fact, the whole event felt a bit like therapy for traumatized people. Families drove from very long distances just to have a taste of social life again, to be around people, to find out answers concerning what the heck happened in this now windswept country of ours. You could see the tragedy and hope in people's eyes. I had people I've never met break down in tears in my presence just from the happiness of the brief end to the isolation they've felt for months. Children were particularly thrilled to go without the muzzle for a few days and have friends with whom to run and play.

Phil Magness delivered a masterful presentation of his research on the failed history of Covid-19 modeling. His focus was on the main proponent of lockdown: the now famous but daily discredited Neil Ferguson and his wild predictions of many millions dead. He more than anyone was responsible for setting off a bandwagon effect of lockdowns that came to the UK and the US, policies which had no significant effects on cases or deaths, wrecked the businesses and lives of millions, hallowed out hospitals with the banning of elective surgeries, and ended up distracting medical professionals from the one thing they could have done to have reduced the death toll: focus on the nursing homes that accounted for 43% of American deaths.[58]

I've seen trolls online call the Porcfest event, Covidfest, but this is just ridiculous. In New Hampshire, in particular, 80% of deaths from Covid-19 occurred among the population living in long-term care facilities. According to the CDC, fully 91% of 311 deaths in the state from Covid-19 have been from among people over 65 years of age with

---

58 The *New York Times*. 2020. "More Than 40% of U.S. Coronavirus Deaths Are Linked to Nursing Homes." *The New York Times*. Accessed June, 2020.

underlying health issues.[59]

Think what that means: the statistical probability, based on known data, that attendees to Porcfest could die from getting Covid-19 approaches zero. And yet, the organizers still faced restrictions on what kinds of businesses could be there and mandates to hand out condescending leaflets on social distancing and so on. And yet the conference went on. That alone served as great inspiration to everyone present: we have to take back our lives from the lockdowners.

I was thrilled to be granted a full two hours for my talk, in which I shared everything I've learned these last months on the history of viruses, pandemic policy in the United States, and the origins of the lockdowns in 2006 during the presidency of George W. Bush. This was the turning point for the Centers for Disease Control, and the real beginning of the politicization of disease. The modelers prevailed over the medical professionals and Bush ordered the CDC to adopt its policies to include shutdown, closures, and lockdowns. It was a tragic moment against which the medical professional protested with passion and wisdom.[60]

For fourteen years, these plans have been sitting there, ready to be deployed, during which time, the virus hobbyist Bill Gates and his money boosted lockdown theory and the view that the only way to achieve herd immunity is through a vaccine, as if there were no such thing as natural or acquired immunity at all. All of this was put in place without any serious concern for things like freedom, prosperity, peace, or social functioning. It was a mad and immoral social experiment and we see the results fully predicted by the medical professionals back in 2006:

Experience has shown that communities faced with epidemics or other adverse events respond best and with the least anxiety when the normal social functioning of the community is least disrupted. Strong political and public health leadership to provide reassurance and to ensure provision of

59 CDC. 2020. "Provisional COVID-19 Death Counts by Sex, Age, and State." *Centers for Disease Control and Prevention.* As of June 29, 2020.

60 Stringham, Edward Peter. 2020. "How a Free Society Deals with Pandemics, According to Legendary Epidemiologist and Smallpox Eradicator Donald Henderson." *American Institute for Economic Research*, May 21.

needed medical care services are critical elements. If either is seen to be less than optimal, a manageable epidemic could move toward catastrophe.

Catastrophe is a pretty good term to describe where we are today. And yet if you turn on the television you can see that the whole discussion has turned from deaths due to Covid-19 to numbers of cases. The reason for this is deaths are down 90% from their peak. Cases are indeed up, but that was precisely what was supposed to happen under the theory of "flattening the curve."

Does anyone even recall that the purpose here was to push cases into the future somehow to preserve hospital capacity? It was never theorized (back then) that hiding from a virus makes it go away. Moreover, the cases we are seeing today are overwhelmingly among young people for whom this virus is hardly a disease at all. Looking at the media hysterics right now, you almost get the impression that certain people do not want this virus to go away the way most viruses do: people acquire immunities to them.

All that aside, we used to speak of this country as the land of the free and home of the brave. Our response to this virus has sacrificed freedom based on fear. Rather than focusing on the actual problem — vulnerable people in nursing homes, many of which were actually forced to take in Covid-19 patients — we shut down nearly the whole country for absolutely no reason.

I recall the first time I attended Porcfest. I was amazed at what I saw. These are people for whom freedom is not just a theoretical parlor game played by intellectuals. Freedom for the people at this event is something that is embraced as a life principle, something to be applied with bravery, determination, and joy. By holding the event this year, Porcfest kept its great tradition. And made a huge contribution to many people's lives: for many, it was the only normal thing they had experienced in the three months since March.

What Good Comes from this Tragedy?

Many millions of people have spent the last four months in sadness and depression. It's hard to watch the world shattered by the bad behavior of governments – and to see too many among us cheer the destruction – and not feel a sense of despair. And yet the human mind is an incredible thing. If we work at it, we can figure out a good takeaway from terrible events. Doing so – it takes effort – can brighten the spirits and point the way forward out of the morass. I've taken three positives out of this experience.

First, I'm completely over my decades-old addiction to news. I always loved the news, even from when I was a kid. For years, I read the *Washington Post* with my morning coffee. Then I switched to the *New York Times*, and learned how to tease truth out of their biased but comprehensive coverage. Then I added the *Wall Street Journal*. When home assistants came along, I programmed mine to play 8 hours (if I needed it) of nonstop news: *BBC, NPR, NYT*, and so many others. It felt like such a luxury. The turning point came for me on February 28, 2020, when the *New York Times* podcast (which used to be my favorite) sent out a piece of panic porn that predicted that the coronavirus would kill 6.6 million Americans, or "six of your friends."

It came as a shock suddenly to realize that they turned over their main podcast to whipping up a public fear to back a lockdown. Explicitly. This was the agenda. They more or less admitted it. I knew at that moment that the paper had signed up to contribute to a malicious plot to enact an unprecedented social/political experiment. The *Times* led the way. Pretty soon, the mainstream media became universally pro-lockdown, probably for political reasons. A widespread and mild virus, dangerous mostly to a particular demographic with low life expectancy and nearly harmless to everyone else, was rendered daily and hourly as a new bubonic plague.

I might have listened for a couple of more days. Then I stopped. The scales fell from my eyes. I decided, suddenly and shockingly for me, to stop filling my head with nonsense. The "news" was not getting me information to help me understand the world; it was clouding my ability to think clearly. A few months later, like clockwork, the revolution at the *New York Times* was complete when its opinion editor, hired to diversify the opinions in the paper, was unceremoniously fired for diversifying opinion in the paper.[61] (The critical theory crowd has discovered new love for the right of institutions to fire people, contradicting decades of left-wing opposition to the same.)

I started getting my information by digging for it, finding reliable accounts on Twitter to follow, spending my time on statistical pages, and otherwise finding facts, reading history, and educating myself more deeply rather than just trusting the media. With one exception: the *Wall Street Journal*, which performed heroically throughout.[62] At this point, I can say that I'm never going back. My addiction to "the news" is over. I'm better off for it. It was painful but I'm glad.

You may be thinking: it's about time. The news has always been about getting eyes and ears and selling advertising. It's just entertainment. It became especially true with the 24-hour news cycle. I don't disagree. I should have given it up years ago. Even now, I can almost immediately tell the difference between a person who watches TV news or listens to mainstream radio vs. those are actually informed about what's going on. In any case, I count this as a real victory, courtesy of the lockdown.

Second, I've saved a tremendous amount of money from not going to restaurants, bars, and movies. I'm sad for all the places that have closed. It's unjust and evil. But from my own perspective, I've learned to live a

---

61 Tracy, Marc. 2020. "James Bennet Resigns as *New York Times* Opinion Editor." *The New York Times*, June 7.

62 Stringham, Edward Peter. 2020. "A Tribute to the *Wall Street Journal's* Editorial Page." *American Institute for Economic Research*, May 11.

good life while spending probably 30% less than I did before. I've fallen back in love with cooking, homespun cocktails, and reading. It's all to the good. I doubt that I will go back, now that I can make all my favorite meals at a fraction of the price I used to pay. Now that things are opening, I perhaps will make my way out to some restaurants but I doubt I will ever go back to the way things were.

Third, I've learned a hugely valuable lesson that civilization can be dismantled in a matter of months. It can happen again if there are not passionate voices out there who understand its basis and can defend it with intellectual integrity, facts, and rhetorical power. I never imagined that anything like this could happen. I thought it was impossible with a Constitution, a tradition of liberty, and a people who would never allow human rights to be taken away so suddenly and cruelly. It did happen, and knowing this has given me renewed passion for my lifetime project of loving, understanding, and spreading the idea of liberty.

It's remarkable how it all happened. The government and its champions took on a subject about which the public is today largely ignorant and fearful – a virus and the claim that 8.25 million Americans will die – and exploited that ignorance to cause people to give up their rights. Even though this whole thing was mapped out 14 years ago, perhaps as a way of finding some rationale for continued and growing presence of government in our lives despite its otherwise growing irrelevance, many on the pro-liberty side of things were caught off guard and didn't know how to respond.

Many people – even people employed with the job of "promoting liberty" – just went silent. For months. Just when their voices were most needed. That was a tragedy. I'll be forever grateful to the pages of AIER which at times in these months felt like a lone voice of sanity out there.[63]

This third lesson – to be grateful for our liberties and civilization and never think they can be taken for granted – is perhaps the most valuable. I'm thinking too that my experience in learning these lessons is not unique. I suspect that many intelligent people have lost faith in the news, rediscovered frugality, and found a new way to commit themselves to the

---

63 Yang, Ethan. 2020. "Smash the COVID Orthodoxy." *American Institute for Economic Research*, July 4.

defense of liberty and human rights. In the coming days, we are going to need stronger and smarter minds to fight the battles of the future. These terrible months might have been the preparation we need to make sure that truth and freedom eventually prevail.

The Day First-World Problems
Became Real

Ten years ago or so, a popular meme spread on the Internet called 'first-world problems.' The idea here is to poke fun at how much we've been spoiled by prosperity and convenience, and how odd it is that we still find things about which to complain. Nothing can go wrong and yet we see wrong things all around us. It is a spin on the fallacy of relative privation, the habit of reveling in fake suffering with a subtext that we have it all ridiculously good.

"My laptop is running out of battery power but the charger is in the next room, so I have to get up from the sofa and trek across the house like a peasant."

"The CVS had 48 brands of toothpaste but not the precise one I wanted, so it's like wartime Russia."

And so on.

You get the idea. It's all fun and charming and speaks to the truth. We'll never fully appreciate the benevolence of the wealth the market economy has bequeathed us and we'll never stop complaining that we don't have enough. And yet these complaints serve a purpose of revealing fixable parts of the imperfect world. A great example are the Clorox wipes that are in every American home now. They didn't exist 20 years ago. You had to mix up a liquid with water and get some rags and later wash them like some medieval serf. Now you just pop a top and get only what you need and throw away the one-time use rag. Beautiful.

Another feature of these first-world problem memes is an underlying presumption that things can only get better from here. There's no real danger of a sudden loss of prosperity or access to wealth. We are so rich

that nothing can hurt us. We can ostentatiously complain in silly ways
without somehow jinxing our privileges. Our status as rich is as unques-
tionable as it is impossible to reverse. With our permanent prosperity, we
are condemned to forever complain about petty things.

That was before the weirdest and wickedest event of our lives, the
lockdowns, upended everything we thought to be true about the world
around us. Just nearly overnight, our trips were cancelled. Schools were
forcibly closed. We faced state-to-state travel restrictions. We could not
use medical services unless we had a specific disease. Bars, restaurants,
retail shops, and normal life itself went away. The lockdowns were enforced
by bureaucrats, police, SWAT teams, with a cheering media that never
stopped lecturing us to obey our masters, comply for purposes of health,
trust the experts, and forget about our so-called rights.

The first two weeks were dominated by shock and awe. Then the despair
set in, along with the drinking, drug use, depression, suicide, and a general
sense that the whole world shifted in ways we can only associate with
nightmare, except that we couldn't wake up from it. Each day was worse
than the previous one. All that we had taken for granted seemed gone.
We only wished we could have our first-world problems back.

We faced something none of us ever imagined: a nationwide shortage
of toilet paper. Stores feared being accused of price gouging and weren't
yet keen on other forms of rationing, so the stuff flew off the shelves.
For weeks, people started conserving in extreme ways. The *New York
Times* deigned to tell us that we shouldn't be using toilet paper anyway.[64]
Then the hand sanitizer went away. And the Clorox wipes. Selected other
products randomly disappeared: rice, pasta, canned soups, chicken (easy
to freeze), paper towels, and so on. You never knew from one day to the
next what would be in the store. There were rumours of food shortages,
and hoarding was going on everywhere.

We dealt with unthinkable and universal stay-at-home orders, even as
the evidence was pouring in that hospitals did not face a capacity problem,
that the real virus danger was heavily focused on one demographic, and

---

64 Murphy, Kate. 2020. "Stop Using Toilet Paper." *The New York Times*, April 3.

it was never clear that the virus is commonly passed asymptomatically. Then the ranks of the unemployed grew to 40 million, and businesses all over the country closed permanently. The blowback, I predicted on April 24, 2020, would ultimately reject social distancing.

What I had not expected is the form it would take: not just hand shaking and hanging out but explosive mass global protests on the streets against the police state. It was a ferocious blowback and it was all over the world. The media had to approve if only to reinforce a priority narrative concerning race. Suddenly in an instant all the finger-wagging demands that we stay home to save lives became celebrations of street protests for justice and equality. It was truly hard to believe. The hypocrisy screamed so loudly that it was impossible to overlook.

Then you have the strange case of Wisconsin, which descended into totalitarianism before the court order on May 12, 2020, to repeal every bit of the lockdown decrees. They were gone in hours and people poured into the bars. Looking at the results, some economists writing at the National Bureau of Economic Research (NBER) discovered: no increased infections or death.[65] The implications are profound but something most of us have come to suspect: the entirety of the destruction of the last months was pointless.

The same happened with the protests: following mass social closening in Minnesota, infections in the state continued to drop.[66] It is almost as if the state took the phrase "herd immunity" literally.

I would only add this: our first-world problems are no longer a laughing matter. We've learned that government can and will destroy our prosperity and rights under the smallest pretext. We can no longer take our freedom and opportunities for granted. We must work unrelentingly to get back what we had and make sure we lock down our governments so that nothing like this will ever happen again.

---

65 Dave, Dhaval M., Andrew I. Friedson, Kyataro Matsuzawa, Drew McNichols, Joseph J. Sabia. 2020. "Did the Wisconsin Supreme Court Restart a COVID-19 Epidemic? Evidence from a Natural Experiment." *NBER Working Paper,* no. 27322.

66 Fink, Jenni. 2020. "Two Weeks After Protests Over George Floyd's Death Began, New Coronavirus Cases in Minnesota Continue to Drop." *Newsweek,* June 10.

Delayed Medical Procedures: Stories from the Front Lines

There was a bit of a chill in my right molar. My left molar was already capped after a root canal. So I wondered if the same was happening on the other side. I called some local dentists. None were in operation but for emergencies and mine didn't qualify. They said they would be opening in a few weeks but only for established patients. I'm not among them. No problem, I thought. I will visit my mother in another state and go to a dentist there. No luck: there was a mandatory two-week quarantine for out-of-state visitors. I couldn't be there waiting for two weeks. Plus, when one of these teeth starts to go bad, as I recall, you are in severe pain within a few days. I could ask my mother to lie for me, but that's not nice.

Fortunately, it was a false alarm and my tooth was fine. Even so, it was scary. Imagine living in a world in which essential dentistry was forbidden by governments for six months. It's like living in the 18th century, or the 12th. Unbelievable.

It's not just about dentistry. By executive orders around the country, all nonessential medical procedures were ended to preserve hospital capacity around the country. It was part of the pandemic plan, *don't you know.* This was also the reason for "flattening the curve" and "social distancing." Hospitals can't scale, *don't you know.* The planners know what's best.

Then something strange happened. All over the country, hospitals emptied, waiting and waiting for floods of Covid-19 patients but few arrived. Only in parts of New York City did resources become temporarily thin. Elsewhere in the country, hospitals almost entirely stopped doing business. Then the financial crisis hit. So far, 266 hospitals have furloughed workers.[67] Then you have the enormous problem of delayed treatments, postponed checkups, bypassed diagnostics – all the things we use the medical system for on a normal basis.

The results are explained in detail by Zaria Gorvett:[68]

> Across the globe, patients have reported being denied cancer care, kidney dialysis and urgent transplant surgeries, with sometimes fatal results.[69] In the Balkans, women have been driven to try dangerous, experimental abortions themselves, while experts in the UK have reported a rise in DIY dentistry, as people turn to toe-curling improvisations involving chewing gum, wire-cutters, and superglue.[70] Panic-hoarding of the drug hydroxychloroquine...has led to shortages.[71]
>
> And as with all crises, the current pandemic looks set to hit the poorest countries the hardest. Scientists have warned that, in some places, disruption to the control of diseases such as HIV, tuberculosis and malaria could lead to losses on the same scale as those caused directly by the virus.[72] Similarly, experts

---

67 Paavola, Alia. 2020. "266 hospitals furloughing workers in response to COVID-19." *Becker's Hospital Review*, April 7.

68 Gorvett, Zaria. 2020. "Why most Covid-19 deaths won't be from the virus." *BBC*, May 28.

69 The Lancet Oncology. 2020. "COVID-19: global consequences for oncology." *The Lancet*, 21(4): 467; Ghosh, Somrita. 2020. "Dialysis patient denied treatment in Delhi, dies." *The New Indian Express*, April 16; Hixenbaugh, Mike. 2020. "'A death sentence': Critically ill patients denied transplants amid coronavirus outbreak." *NBC News*, March 18.

70 Sinoruka, Fjori, Ana Curic, and Francesca Visser. 2020. "Balkans women face closed clinics and unsafe abortions under COVID-19." *OpenDemocracy*, May 6; Mintz, Luke. 2020. "Chewing gum, wire-cutters, and superglue: the alarming rise of DIY Dentistry under coronavirus." *The Telegraph*, May 18.

71 Callahan, Mary. 2020. "Drug for autoimmune disorders in short supply because of diversion to COVID-19 cases, where it's unproven to help." *The Press Democrat*, April 10.

72 Hogan, Alexandra B., Britta Jewell, Ellie Sherrard-Smith, Juan Vesga, Oliver J Watson et al. 2020. "Report 19: The Potential Impact of the COVID-19 Epidemic on HIV, TB and Malaria in Low- and Middle-Income Countries." *Imperial College COVID-19 Response Team.*

fear that deaths from illnesses such as cholera could far exceed those from Covid-19 itself. [73]

Vaccinations are a particular concern. The World Health Organization has calculated that at least 80 million children under the age of one are now at risk of diphtheria, polio and measles, after the pandemic disrupted programmes in at least 68 countries.[74] Polio is expected to make a comeback, despite a multi-billion dollar effort stretching back decades which meant it was tantalisingly close to joining the exclusive club of viruses that are extinct in the wild, whose sole member is currently smallpox.[75]

The tragedies here are countless, and should have been expected. If you impose a governor's plan over the experience of hospital management, and do so under a coercive threat, in the name of public health, you are likely going to see the opposite emerge. So I asked my Twitter feed for some examples. Many I can't share due to privacy concerns but here are just a few:

Just before "lockdown" I had abdominal pain and days of constipation. (Wish my issue was more glamorous.) I saw the lockdown looming so I went to the emergency room (March 11, 2020). Diagnosed with diverticulitis. Given antibiotics, for the abdominal infection, and referred to a Gastroenterologist for a colonoscopy. I keep attempting to make the appointment for the colonoscopy and they are telling me to try to schedule again at the beginning of June. In the meantime I have been

73 Hoffman, Jan. 2020. "Polio and Measles Could Surge After Disruption of Vaccine Programs." *The New York Times*, May 22.

74 WHO. 2020. "At least 80 million children under one at risk of diseases such as diphtheria, measles and polio as COVID-19 disrupts routine vaccination efforts, warn Gavi, WHO and UNICEF." *World Health Organization (WHO)*, May 22.

75 Lahariya, Chandrakant. 2007. "Global eradication of polio: the case for 'finishing the job.'" *Bulletin of the World Health Organization*, 85(6): 421-500; WHO. 2020. "Does polio still exist? Is it curable?" *World Health Organization*, January 20.

trying to get my body to keep things moving by taking laxatives at times. I went 100 hours without a bowel movement.

I think I am getting my body back into a good routine. I can still go to work and play disc golf most of the time. So it's not debilitating 95% of the time. I've lost 15 pounds (flattening my curve). I imagine much more serious issues occurring for others.

———

I fractured my collarbone in a road bike crash in May 2018. Being in Canada, I had to wait several painful days before surgery was scheduled to fix a metal plate to the broken bone. I was told that it was possible to have the plate removed after approximately six months when the bone would have healed. The discomfort from the plate rubbing under the skin, and from the tension of 9 screws in the small bone, made it an easy decision to request surgery to remove the plate.

My surgeon added my name to the waiting list in January 2019. At the time he said the average wait was about five months. After six months, I phoned the hospital and was told that I was still on the list but that they were scheduling people who had been on it for over a year. I was finally contacted in March 2020(!) with a date two weeks later for the surgery. The day before, they called to ask if I had been out of the country or in contact with anyone who had been during the previous two weeks. The answer was yes, so they cancelled the surgery and said they would call me back. I'm still waiting.

———

I have extreme sciatica pain and my pain doctor after months has determined that I need a nerve block in my sacrum. This is an injection that literally can be done in less than ten minutes, but I have had to wait over 8 weeks in excruciating pain while they wait to get me in after the backlog in elective surgeries. They refuse to give me opioids.

———

Not my personal story, but comes from our lawn care folks, a husband and wife team. She had a wisdom tooth that was pushing up too much and starting to be bothersome, and she had an appointment scheduled to have it removed. Then along comes COVID, and all non-essential medical treatments, including teeth extractions, are cancelled by executive fiat. (We are in Michigan, so this is Gretchen Whitmer, our governor who issued this order). Anyway, the tooth kept bothering her. In short order an abscess forms, which goes septic, which leaks into her bloodstream. Oral antibiotics do not seem to cut it, and she ends up in ICU in hospital for 17 days on IV antibiotics.

I just spoke to her husband this morning, and she is now home though still very weak. According to him the hospital thought she was about 10 hours away from dying before they found the antibiotic combination that seemed to work.

Also anecdotal, our neighbors have two doctors in the family. One of them, a pediatrician, told me last week that basically he was bored because he had nothing to do with all non-essential appointments cancelled. The other one, an ER resident, told us that the word in the University of Michigan hospital system was that they are on track to lose about a billion dollars in Q1 of 2020.

———

I've had a knee meniscus surgery delayed because of the virus, as well as follow up treatment for my recently operated on knee.

This is only a small look. An informal poll of my friends shows that almost everyone has faced some kind of delay or neglect, as a medical system designed to deal with such problems came to be victimized by the shutdowns.

God help you if you had a stroke over these months.[76]

New research published on May 28, 2020, in the *Journal of NeuroInterventional Surgery* (JNIS) shows ischemic stroke patients are arriving at hospitals and treatment centers an average of 160 minutes later during the Covid-19 pandemic, as compared with a similar time frame in 2019. These delays, say stroke surgeons from the Society of NeuroInterventional Surgery (SNIS), are impacting both survival and recovery.

Then there was another problem: the fear of the hospitals themselves.[77]

"The hospital was an ominous, nerve-racking and scary place for patients even before Covid," said Dr. Lisa VanWagner, a transplant hepatologist at Northwestern Medicine in Chicago. "Now you take a stressful situation like a pandemic and you tell people that they cannot have their normal support system while they're in the hospital, and that really magnifies those fears."

The issue of delayed medical care, like countless others, was never mentioned in the glorified plans that public health professionals cobbled together over the last 14 years. They also failed to account for other major consequences, such as the psychological toll of being treated like animals, or riots in the streets.

The history of central planning is replete with failure. The lesson pertains in every area of life, not excluding matters of public health.[78] One might think we would learn from the past rather than continuing to conduct such experiments with people's lives.

76 News Medical. 2020. "Research finds delayed treatment for ischemic stroke patients during COVID-19 pandemic." *News Medical Life Sciences*, May 28.

77 Hafner, Katie. 2020. "Fear of Covid-19 Leads Other Patients to Decline Critical Treatment." *The New York Times*, May 25.

78 Hart, David. 2020. "Pandemic Policy in One Page." *American Institute for Economic Research*, May 29.

Lockdown Suicide Data Reveal
Predictable Tragedy

On March 28, 2020, the American Institute for Economic Research ran a terrifying article that didn't receive the attention it deserved, even though the research behind it was impeccable and detailed. It was "Drugs, Suicide, and Crime: Empirical Estimates of the Human Toll of the Shutdown."[79] On suicide in particular, the article said the following:

> Whether it is the direct unemployment effect or the potential poverty produced from the economic shutdown that leads to greater suicides, an increase from the 48,344 suicides and 1,400,000 suicide attempts in the US in 2018 should give decision-makers pause during their response to this pandemic.[80]

That article created in me a sense of dread. The warning was issued but unheeded. And sure enough, we now read that "California doctors say they've seen more deaths from suicide than coronavirus since lockdowns."[81]

> "The numbers are unprecedented," Dr. Mike deBoisblanc of John Muir Medical Center in Walnut Creek, California, told *ABC 7*

---

79 Redford, Audrey, and Thomas K. Duncan. 2020. "Drugs, Suicide, and Crime: Empirical Estimates of the Human Toll of the Shutdown." *American Institute for Economic Research*, March 28.

80 AFSP. 2020. "Suicide statistics." *American Foundation for Suicide Prevention (AFSP)*, March.

81 Miller, Andrew Mark. 2020. "California doctors say they've seen more deaths from suicide than coronavirus since lockdowns." *Washington Examiner*, May 21.

News about the increase of suicide deaths adding that he's seen a "year's worth of suicides" in the last four weeks alone.[82]

DeBoisblanc said he believes it's time for California officials to end the stay-at-home order and let people back out into their communities.

"Personally, I think it's time," he said. "I think, originally, this was put in place to flatten the curve and to make sure hospitals have the resources to take care of COVID patients. We have the current resources to do that, and our other community health is suffering."

Kacey Hansen, a trauma center nurse at John Muir Medical Center for over 30 years, says she's not only worried about the increased suicide attempts but also about the hospital's ability to save as many patients as usual.

"What I have seen recently, I have never seen before," Hansen said. "I have never seen so much intentional injury."…

By late March, more people had died in just one Tennessee county from suicide than had died in the entire state directly from the virus.[83] Data out of Arizona show a similar trend.[84] I'm thinking that you know many people who have privately admitted to you that they have variously entered into a dark place during these times. Unemployment and having your bank account drained can do that.

It's not just about money. Even if material provision is present, the sudden loss of freedom and life-control is demoralizing and debilitating. We have always taken it for granted in America that we are in charge of our own futures. Then one day, without warning, without consultation of voters, without votes from legislatures, it was all gone. Schools, bars,

---

82 Hollyfield, Amy. 2020. "Suicides on the rise amid stay-at-home order, Bay Area medical professionals say." *ABC 7 News*, May 21.

83 Mastrangelo, Dominick. 2020. "Suicides outpacing coronavirus deaths in Tennessee, data says." *Washington Examiner*, March 29.

84 Vernachio, Veronika. 2020. "Suicide rates spike through COVID-19 pandemic." *KGUN 9*, May 19.

gyms, parks, and whole cities were forcibly shut by executive edict, all in the name of virus control with precious little thought put to the costs or legal protections we believed were in place to protect our freedom and property. Zoom became our social outlet – and it's a very poor substitute for the real thing. Life's purpose became unclear.

Which is what makes this *New York Times* headline so preposterous: Is the Pandemic Sparking Suicide?[85]

Is the Pandemic Sparking Suicide?

Psychiatrists are confronted with an urgent natural experiment, and the outcome is far from predictable.

The pandemic did this? The content alone shows that fear of disease pales in comparison to economic hardship in driving suicide. In addition, there is another huge factor: mandatory social separation is a psychological disaster.

> "It's a natural experiment, in a way," said Matthew Nock, a psychology professor at Harvard. "There's not only an increase in anxiety, but the more important piece is social isolation." He added, "We've never had anything like this — and we know social isolation is related to suicide."

So, yes, this can generate terrifying but predictable results. Again, the problem is material but, more profoundly, it is spiritual. Lockdowns crush dreams, impose a loss of control, separate you from friends, surround people with police ready to arrest you for doing what only a few days earlier was perfectly normal and legal. It just didn't seem possible that something like this could happen in America. But it did.

At the same time, we are profoundly aware that many people have been enthusiastic participants in lockdown culture. Given the scant science and

---

85 Carey, Benedict. 2020. "Is the Pandemic Sparking Suicide?" *The New York Times*, May 19.

medical evidence that they save lives, that they are actually achieving the goal, how can we account for the many people who not only did not enter into a dark place but rather found new purpose through them?[86]

I draw your attention to a neglected classic: *War Is a Force that Gives Us Meaning* by Chris Hedges.[87] Hedges was a foreign affairs correspondent for the *New York Times*, and travelled the world covering war zones in Latin America, Sudan, and other hotspots. He began to notice a pattern in modern war. It not only rattled front-line soldiers. It shook entire societies and corrupted everyone. Everyone in society was dragged into it, many on the side of the state and believing that they were on a eschatological mission to defeat evil. They turned against dissidents and those who are insufficiently enthusiastic.

"The communal march against an enemy generates a warm, unfamiliar bond with our neighbors, our community, our nation, wiping out unsettling undercurrents of alienation and dislocation," he writes. He concludes that in societies where regular life and peace seemed to lack meaning for people, war gives them that meaning and purpose.

This book keeps coming back to me when people ask how it is that these lockdowns seem to have enjoyed some measure of public support, at least in the first month or so. It's a difficult question to answer since human beings don't usually welcome being treated like animals and pushed around with billy clubs and sprayed with mace when they resist. On the other hand, violence, shock, and awe can feel temporarily satisfying and meaningful for people who have otherwise lost a sense of life purpose.

These days in which I'm writing feel very good as compared with the last six months. People are coming to their senses and things are opening up. So many people have said something to me about how they are "so over this." Good. I'm also receiving fewer calls from friends who are despondent. Maybe the worst is over.

And yet that data will be pouring in for many months and years:

86 Tucker, Jeffrey A. 2020. "Did the Lockdown Save Lives?" *American Institute for Economic Research*, May 19.

87 Hedges, Chris. 2002. *War Is a Force that Gives Us Meaning*. Public Affairs.

suicides, overdoses, domestic abuse, and every manner of social pathology. It was predicted and predictable. And tragically, many businesses that could help in the mental-health recovery process have closed due to the lockdown.[88] For years we will be left with the question of why. It's too early for final answers, but the question will haunt us for the rest of our lives.

---

88 Dobrowolski, Tony. 2020. "Kripalu to lay off 450, shut down until 2021." *The Berkshire Eagle*, May 21.

"I've Lost Faith in Humanity": The Psychological Toll of the Lockdown

We have heretofore lived our lives with the presumption that we possess the inalienable right to choose. We are self-governors, the main masters of our domains. Our lives are what we make of them. We can improve, act, and see results. We craft our futures. We can travel, save or spend, work here or there, be this person or that, move, love, practice religion or not, dress up or down, drink liquor or not, have children or not and care for them in the way we think best, and generally be in charge of our lives within the limit of the law.

That is to say, we have presumed that we are basically free. We had purpose, direction, and a future. In the course of a mere three days in March of 2020, most of that was taken away from us. Government executives took over without the mandate from legislatures or the people. They made a mockery of every slogan from American history: government by the people and for the people, land of the free and home of the brave, sweet land of liberty, and so on.

The media blared new slogans at us about distancing, flattening, sheltering, and then it started closing up almost everything we think of as the substance of the good life. We were locked in our homes, forcibly separated from friends and family and even faith. They killed commercial society. They killed choice. They killed freedom.

Everything we supposed was true about our lives was smashed under foot, enforced by new police states that sprang up around us, while the media urged even more stringent controls and the US president foundered in endless press conferences and shifting policies, while the US Congress threw away many trillions in tax dollars. Practically overnight, we were reduced by states to sheltering animals with only the privilege to go to the grocery store to snag our next meal to eat at home, while otherwise having our liberty and property being slaughtered by governing officials.

On March 28, 2020, AIER warned of a coming wave of drug overdoses, domestic abuse cases, and suicides, based on existing empirical literature on unemployment and sudden financial crisis.[89] However, that's only the most conspicuous result. There is also the less-obvious way into which the shutdowns eat away at our hearts, spirits, and souls.

In the days since, I've sensed an existential crisis that compares for me only to the time I was thrown behind bars for the failure to pay a speeding ticket and found myself in the strange position of relying on favors from people who cared nothing about me while being cut off from everyone I love. That experience changed me forever, such that I never again took my freedom for granted. All of America has gone through this now, not just for one day but for a ghastly six weeks in which our freedom and rights as human beings have been taken away.

I've read in F.A.Hayek when he noted that the most horrible toll of wartime statism was psychological, "an alteration in the character of the people." He describes the feeling of being treated like a cog in a machine and how that leaves us all feeling thoroughly dehumanized. I've noticed this happening to friends of mine, who in these awful Zoom hangouts we have suddenly started breaking down into tears of desperation.

And so I asked people on my Twitter feed to tell their stories. My inbox has been suddenly flooded with an outpouring of desperate sadness, rage, shock, and horror. I can only share some with you here. I have changed any details that might violate their privacy rights.

———

I've struggled with depression for a long time. Last September I intentionally overdosed on several prescriptions. I was comatose

---

89 Redford, Audrey, & Thomas K. Duncan. 2020. "Drugs, Suicide, and Crime: Empirical Estimates of the Human Toll of the Shutdown." *American Institute for Economic Research*, March 28.

for 3 days. Initially, my parents were told that I wouldn't survive but after a couple days I held in there. The doctors then believed that I would be severely brain damaged. And when I first woke up I couldn't remember my name, age, or birthday. I couldn't walk or speak in full sentences. By God's grace I was discharged on the 6th day with my mental faculties restored but with some physical challenges. I spent time with family and friends and in therapy building my support system, creating a healthy lifestyle of coping skills, and learning how to prevent myself from being so isolated and devoid of hope.

With the lockdown, it feels as though every step of progress as well as every healthy avenue of support was ripped from me via government fiat. Church, socializing, therapy/support groups, even the very outdoors were no longer at my disposal to help me in this time when I needed them most. All of my family is out of state and I cannot get to anyone due to the various state lockdowns. I'm isolated, powerless, and in despair which is a dangerous recipe for me.

I'm doing what I have to in order to make it through. But it's an upward battle against the seemingly unending nature of the lockdowns, deep loss of control over my daily life, and the maddening sense that my freedom is not only subject to local despots but also the whims of the public who cheer on tyranny and shout down any suggestion of liberty. In my darkest moments I pray to understand why I survived only for this ongoing nightmare to become my reality. My faith brings some comfort but I struggle with despair and anger every day.

Hopefully soon the public will realize that government action has created more victims than an already scary situation needed.

––––

I got depressed, again, riding through the downtown area of my small, southern hometown yesterday, which usually would be packed with folks walking between the pubs and restaurants, or sitting outside sampling beer and food while listening to a free band in "The Alley," enjoying a cool, breezy spring day. Instead it was empty, as it has been for almost two months now. The thoughts that plague my mind the most are: How can we throw it all away so easily? Did everyone not read Steinbeck's *The Grapes Of Wrath* in school? Did everyone not "pledge allegiance to the flag" daily? Does everyone not know the history of the 20th century, and understand how precious liberty is? Do people have no reverence for the blood and treasure that was spent to secure liberty to ourselves and other countries?

We're literally tearing down everything that mankind has built. Everyone tells me that "the economy will bounce right back," but they haven't read Hayek, Sowell, von Mises, or Tucker. Obviously, it doesn't work that way. Maybe it's because I drove a truck for 20 years, and saw firsthand the vast factories and warehouses all over the US and Canada, and quickly gained an appreciation for logistics and how the whole world is connected, and how fragile it all really is, which most people never really see unless there is the temporary delay due to a hurricane or snowstorm.

I miss going to the gym. Even though I'm currently not drinking, I miss going to the bar and shooting pool with my brother and the few friends I have. I miss the plays at our community theatre and who knows when the local symphony will ever play again at our small state university branch?

As I read another article today about the impending meat shortages, the thought struck me, again, that people really don't understand what's coming; they never understood how their groceries magically appear on the shelves, and I don't understand how we could just throw it all away. Rand and Orwell warned us, but we didn't listen.

———

I have been very concerned, saddened, and even angry over the past few weeks about the sudden loss of freedom. I've been even more concerned that it seems many people (on the conservative and liberal side) do not seem to care. I love the US of A. I love it because we were the first nation in the history of the world to make all people free. We can pursue whatever careers we want, we can travel around, eat what we like, say what we want, and meet anywhere, anytime. We can worship as we choose, dress as we choose, and live wherever and however we want. This is why the USA is so amazing. This is unheard of in many countries and for the majority of human history.

I have been so sad and disappointed that a single virus has eroded our freedoms basically overnight. Not only is it wrong and unAmerican, it is even unconstitutional. I am scared for the future of the United States, but at the same time, I remain cautiously optimistic at this point. The backlash, complaints, rallys, and cries for freedom get louder and louder. We have a huge change of opinion in the public and people just take back their freedoms. Businesses open up, people go out, and politicians lose more power than they even thought possible. This psychologically is the ideal outcome. Americans get in touch with their roots, take back their country, and resume being in control of their own destiny.

———

By the grace of the universe, I have been spared many of the direct consequences of the lockdown, or the virus itself for that matter. I didn't suffer any deleterious change in my life, only some inconveniences... for now.

Yet I feel like my psychology has been fundamentally altered, for better or worse. I've always suffered from a feeling of isolation. I don't think like other people, I don't accept what I'm told to believe, and I've always had a hard time relating to people because of that. The majority's lazy, careless acceptance of draconian lockdown measures has distanced me even further, to an unsettling degree. I sense my typical asocial personality is growing anti-social.

It's as if I'm being forced to abandon my empathy, which is pretty tough when you pride yourself on it. But if the majority thinks I should be forced to sit home and rot away, inconsiderate of my circumstances, why the hell should I even care what happens to these people, outside of my own self-interests? Although I am not giving in to my emotional, sometimes comical, overreactions, how long will it be before they consume my thoughts? Probably never, luckily. Nonetheless, my antagonism toward humanity grows by the day, and that's scary.

————

My neighbors cannot be trusted to fight for liberty or have a logical debate. I have been yelled at for stating the stats. Someone even threatened to report me. They have fetishized this situation. They have become petulant minions of petty tyrants. They are driven by emotions and have no sense of reason. People are unexpectedly gullible.

I lived in Brazil in the 1990s during their currency crash. I have this sense of doom. It feels like we're going to face 1,000% inflation. No one around me fears this. No one is questioning the printing of money. Indeed, they demand more.

When I do get out to Menards (Home Depot) or the grocer, speakers that used to blast music are blasting talking points and these catchphrases. There are placards everywhere telling me to stay away from other people. It's like living in a B horror film.

This has destroyed my optimism for humanity. We are really controlled by our overlords and a good portion of the public will fall into line. I will have a hard time trusting people again. Isn't this the same sort of thing that gave Hitler so much power? These are the same people that have been screaming that Trump is a dictator, yet they want him to do more.

I also made the mistake of running across evidence of powerful people planning an event *like* this. These people aren't going to leave us alone. I feel like we're being lied to, fed off of and indoctrinated. They are indoctrinated.

I feel stranded on a ship of fools. My sense of humanity is completely destroyed.

––––

While many believe in different levels of freedom, I think many of us took for granted just how many small freedoms we take for granted, things that fall within our sphere of influence.

Something as 'small' as going to a restaurant, or to the movies, (which, in many ways should be considered minor miracles if we look at just how much time people had to spend in drudgery through human history) are things that fall within our intimate control, and where we feel we are in charge of how we spend our time. Any hint of control over our individual spheres was ripped from all of us in the most brutal way.

––––

One thing that keeps recurring in my mind is a conversation I had with one of our son's kung fu instructors. He said that he had heard, or read (I don't know where), that the vast majority of our communication is NOT in the form of our words, but in facial expressions and gestures, even very subtle facial signs that indicate how we are feeling, what we are thinking, etc.

He had done a lot of traveling as a photographer, to many places where he did not speak the language, and talked about his personal experience with this, and about how he had many many "conversations" with people, where they understood each other very well, without speaking the same language.

I keep thinking about this as I see people walking around in their masks (fortunately, fewer are wearing them than even a week ago!) and huddled away in their homes.

———

Everyone around me just goes along with it. I got kicked out of a big box store for not wearing a mask. I can't get a haircut. Is life really worth living if I'm being ordered around by someone I've never met and who doesn't give a damn about me??

I have more money now than I've ever had. And more free time than ever. No real responsibilities or obligations. And yet it feels so… empty. Like it was all for nothing. Extremely sad.

———

I am bipolar with generalized anxiety disorder. The shutdown has drastically increased my anxiety and crippled me with depression such that I can barely put together the effort to teach even the reduced 4 hours a day I do for my high school students. I have it comparatively well, as I haven't lost pay and am working much less nonetheless. Without my massively supportive wife I'm not sure I'd be getting through this.

———

Things are "normal" here compared to reports from friends and family in major metros when at the supermarket. Some mask and glove and some don't, but many of the doctors and nurses here glove and mask every winter regardless. The major industries here are medical, chemical, and scientific research. Manufacturing is second, but distant. We fit all of the stereotypes about meth, opioid addiction, intergenerational poverty, and the intersection of all that with new wealth.

My son is missing his friends desperately and is very upset that many of them are MIA without even a, "We're good, thanks!" from the parents. The poor kid sleeps later and later every day. I have to get him up now. My partner is spending a great deal of time at nursing homes seeing things that are dispiriting enough that he won't talk about them. He comes home defeated and deeply sad.

I'm cracking. My work is suspended indefinitely, but I'd need to be home for my son either way. I've yelled twice this weekend. I've cried privately a few times. My bright spot is that my darling retired 65-year-old parents have moved to a neighboring town to be near us, and they give absolutely no f**** about what is going on. True honey badgers. They grew up in poverty and uncertainty, saw war, did well in spite of everything, and have the ability to see around even big things like this.

———

Hospitals in my state, like many others, are postponing screenings and surgeries because of Covid-19. Well, I was diagnosed with bladder cancer in fall 2019 and it was removed in surgery. (This is an especially rare situation as I am a 34-year-old non-smoking female.)

I had a follow-up screening that was going to be postponed 5 weeks, but I raised a fuss and got my original appointment back. There were two suspicious spots that will need to be biopsied and tested, so thank God we caught them.

If the spots turn out to be cancerous, another 5 weeks could have made things so much worse. As it is, the anxiety of having cancer on top of all that's going on in the country/economy, does plenty of physical and mental damage.

Now I'm waiting to find out when I can get the biopsy, how long the test results will take, and what the next steps will be. Because of how hospitals have responded to Covid-19, I'm afraid that I won't have access to further treatments in time–testing, surgeries, chemotherapy if necessary. If the hospital or health system goes bankrupt, I don't know where that will leave me.

———

My father passed away from Stage 4 cancer last May. My mother had to sell her home after his passing due to probate crap. This has left my 80-year old mother living with us while we build a house for her closer to her kids.

Once the grandkids were forced home from school, she had to move out to a home in the woods 2 hours away. She is isolated and has comorbidities. She's had a cough and her blood pressure is out of control and she is afraid to go to the hospital. Her house build has slowed down. I can only imagine that if my father was still alive, his cancer treatments would be on hold for all of this. Her health is deteriorating and her anxiety intensified.

We are lucky we can afford multiple homes. The problem must be infinitely worse for those who can't. I was lucky to listen to a few of my friends and I bought a bug-out kit that had a case of N95s and other medical gear to help her and other physicians close to us.

Everyone's liberty is now negotiable as long as one immunocompromised person exists on earth.

———

The most damaging toll for me has been the complete blurring of the lines between personal and professional life. My wife and I have both been working at home for six weeks now. We have a toddler and a five-month-old baby. We have childcare a couple of days a week so we are both able to work undistracted, but on the other days there are more distractions than I have ever faced before.

At my office I can compartmentalize, hunker down and get tons of work done, and then go home and have my full attention on family and personal matters. Having the lines blurred I think has resulted in lower quality attention at work and at home. This is more of a comment on damage to objective results than to psychology, but subjectively speaking the lack of clear boundaries has been awful. Work invades home and home invades work.

———

As a parent of three young children this whole experience has been confusing for them and isolating for us. All of our social supports were gone within a span of five days from our local trail life group to church on Sundays... They couldn't even play on the playground for a little while just to burn off some energy. We would drive to a local trail and they would see the caution tape in the gates closed and be very confused. Seeing that made me angry. I have found myself distracted and melancholy. This experience has also left me very disappointed in the great American experiment that something like this can happen so quickly and without really any redress.

———

We did not "lose" anything. It was **taken** from us by people who think they are tasked with doing so. From a psychological standpoint, it fed their megalomania. People like my governor, Andrew Cuomo, have spent the better part of their lives believing they were called to lead. Same with the mayor of New York City. These people believe not only that they know better, but that their **job** is to show it! As for the deep, psychotic version of megalomania and narcissism being experienced by our Comb-Over in Chief in the Oval Office, well, that would take too long to describe!

We are, in effect, hostages. From that standpoint, all this shows is the truth that was already staring us in the face. A**holes — apologies for my choice of words — that we know are barely qualified to operate a toilet, are in position to place mandates on our lives. Victor Frankl and Marcus Aurelius might advise us that how we respond to this situation is more important than what these losers actually do to us. Of course, I agree. However, one additional factor makes this situation all the more dicey. When those around you, the people with whom you actually share the foxhole, not only acquiesce to the wishes of these lunatics, but also become participants in your suffering, that makes it suck all the worse. When people are actually calling tip-lines on their neighbors, and the like, the programming has reached new depths and even the most stoic-thinking among us can only experience supreme despair.

———

I am a single woman, no children, approaching the end of child-bearing age (who wants children?). Prior to October of last year, for the previous three years or so, my father's depression (and self-medication by alcohol) gradually worsened, and I eventually had to cut ties with my parents (my mother enabled by drinking with him). My father was my childhood best friend. He was functionally a brother and father since I am an only child.He gradually faded into a man who was consumed by his feelings of penance (he came from a hyper-religious Mormon family and had lost his brother to alcoholism/depression when I was a sophomore in University — something he blamed himself for, thinking he could have "saved him"), loneliness, lack of purpose, and physical pain. He was increasingly distant, so intoxicated each time I went home that we rarely could have linear, meaningful conversations anymore.

He foreshadowed his own death; said he didn't think he would make it to retirement (62; three years from his fore-shadowing), and it became too much to sit idly by. I severed ties, saw him one last time in July of last year (he was jaundiced and gave me the longest, tightest hug he's ever given me — I'm sure he knew he was ill), and then in October, after a series of kidney issues, he had a MI due to atrial fibrillation, and then was in an induced coma in the hospital, liver had failed, kidneys no longer processing, and the brain damage was so bad from anoxia that he was seizing constantly, his yellowed eyes opening each time. We let him off of life support the following day. He died with my head on his chest. My best friend, gone.

I was let go of my job and offered a severance package the day I returned from bereavement. I accepted as I'd been interviewing. I was offered a new position, for which I needed to move elsewhere, in California. My mom was incapable of organizing a memorial due to feeling overwhelmed — my father had managed everything for our family besides the garden (my mom's thing), so my mom asked if I'd organize a memorial after I moved and started a new job, at some point during the spring.

Then, in early March, California began its series of shutdowns. First, the Bay Area where the tiny condo I owned (that I was desperately trying to rent out) was locked down. People were hesitant to come view the condo due to the shutdown, and many applicants were not financially sound. I drained my bank account in the following months, paying California rent and mortgage, until it was finally rented two weeks ago. The county provisions where my mother lived and where I live prohibit visiting family and any size gatherings, so my grieving mother needed to be alone, in their gang-ridden neighborhood, while I struggled with grieving my father. Then, my pay was cut; 20% across the board at my company (or furloughed). I'm grateful to have a job, but I'm barely hanging on to my job.

I've drained my savings, nothing left to freeze my eggs, no dating, no in-person support groups, and no foreseeable point at which we will be able to host a memorial for my father in the near future. I don't know when my financial situation will be back to normal, and each week, Newsom seems to move the goalposts. First it was to "flatten the curve," then "open the Western states," and now that Oregon is planning on opening, it's a six-point plan that completely disregards the serological work out of USC and Stanford, and even liberal bastions like New York State.

I know this is not the most dramatic story, but it's weighed heavily on my mind since I am surrounded by people more than willing to give away every ounce of freedom and livelihood for an IFR of 0.1% while ignoring the collateral damage of people like me who have suffered mightily with depression and trauma, and the countless others who won't have jobs to go back to.

———

It makes me feel hopeless. No matter what I do or create in life, government can just step in and take it all away. The incentive to be great has shattered. Why be great when your success can just be gone whenever government says so?

———

One of my best friends is gay and he said he's seen more ODs and suicides in his circle within the gay community in the past 4 weeks than in the past few years.

———

I will conclude with the immortal words: never again. Hang in there, my friends, we will clean up the carnage and reclaim what is ours.

Authoritarianism in Auckland

For months we've heard the cry: oh how wonderfully New Zealand dealt with Covid-19. They did the tightest lockdown in the world! The coronavirus – no doubt astonished by the decisiveness and ferocity of Prime Minister Jacinda Ardern, the heroine of all media – just decided not to make this wonderful country a home. The virus was bested by political wit!

But that was a fantasy all along, as Oxford's Sunetra Gupta pointed out from the beginning.[90] All New Zealand did was delay the inevitable. In the modern world, there is no chance for a developed society to replicate the experience of a primitive tribe with naive immune systems living in isolation. You wouldn't want to do that anyway because you make the whole population of your tribe fatally vulnerable to the next bug that comes along. In Gupta's view, New Zealand's "success" wouldn't be that at all.

She also finds New Zealand's approach immoral: a selfish demand that the rest of the world bear the burden of herd immunity while Kiwis hide in their homes and surf the Internet. Indeed, interestingly, she regards the New Zealand policy as a violation of the global social contract — the first truly persuasive deployment of that phrase that I've heard.

Still, after 100 days, the *New York Times* sang a hymn to the country and its leader: "New Zealand's successful fight against COVID-19 has made the Pacific island nation of 5 million one of the safest places in the world right now."[91] People had been going about their business, eating in

---

90 Tucker, Jeffrey A. 2020. "How Global Capitalism Boosted Immunities." *American Institute for Economic Research*, July 25.

91 Menon, Praveen. 2020. "New Zealand Records 100 Days Without Domestic Virus Case but Warns Against Complacency." *Reuters*, August 9.

restaurants and going to movies, while sniffing in disdain at the rest of the world for allowing the virus to sweep through and gain herd immunity. New Zealand found another way! A scientific way!

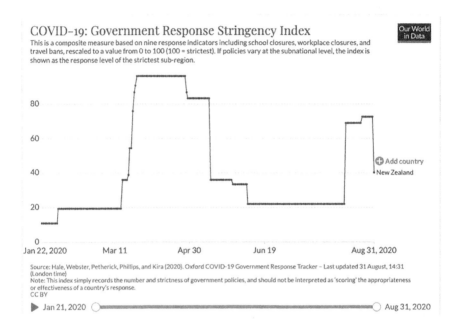

COVID-19: Government Response Stringency Index
This is a composite measure based on nine response indicators including school closures, workplace closures, and travel bans, rescaled to a value from 0 to 100 (100 = strictest). If policies vary at the subnational level, the index is shown as the response level of the strictest sub-region.

Source: Hale, Webster, Petherick, Phillips, and Kira (2020). Oxford COVID-19 Government Response Tracker – Last updated 31 August, 14:31 (London time)
Note: This index simply records the number and strictness of government policies, and should not be interpreted as 'scoring' the appropriateness or effectiveness of a country's response.
CC BY

The upcoming election, proclaimed Ardern the Magnificent, would be a "Covid election." Alas, the virus was not entirely eradicated after all. After going 102 days without a reported case, tests found four people in one family tested positive for Covid-19. Yes, that's 4 people in a city of 1.7 million. I could find nothing on whether they showed symptoms or how severe they were. In any case, if the goal is complete banishment of the virus through an aggressive application of state power, clearly something has to be done. Panic time!

With four cases, what to do? Well, sure enough, Ardern the Great announced a full lockdown in the city of Auckland. Everyone home. All businesses except essentials are closed. Public venues including libraries, museums, cinemas, food courts, gyms, pools, playgrounds and markets will all close as soon as the lockdown begins. Ardern's announcement immediately caused panic buying.[92] Customers blasted past security to load up in preparation for a long period of disaster.

Camelot is now under police-state rule yet again. Road blocks.[93] Delayed elections.[94] After four cases! We await videos of police tackling people to the ground, commandos breaking down doors, restrictions on hoarding groceries, a brutal contact-tracing regime, fines and jails for daring to gather with friends, and all the concomitant side effects of lockdowns: drug overdoses, alcoholism, depression, and suicide. You can observe how much the country locked down and then opened up with a sense of false comfort, only to lock down again. Talk about regime uncertainty!

There was always an issue however. New Zealand's economy relies directly and indirectly on international tourism for 10% of its GDP, and the industry employs 188,000 people. Would it have to end permanently, or perhaps every visitor would be subjected to testing and quarantine forever? That wouldn't exactly be good for business. That's one way to end a dream.

Safe is not the first word to come to mind in the 'safespace' state, where cops are a greater threat to the public than Covid-19.

Here we get to the root problem of lockdown theory. Initially, in the US and UK, it was about curve flattening to preserve hospital capacity. That gradually mutated into a completely different theory that politicians would use police power to suppress and eradicate a virus. To my knowledge – anyone can read a Dummies-style book on viruses on Kindle – no truly competent immunologist would say that suppression is either viable or desirable. And yet to one extent or another, most governments in the world, save a handful, attempted to do just this. We once knew about viruses, and then suddenly, we did not.[95] It has been called the greatest failure of

---

92 Cooper, Luke. 2020. "Coronavirus: Panic buying breaks out in Auckland within hours of New Zealand lockdown announcement." *9 News*, August 11.

93 Lawrence, Kirsty, Ellen O'Dwyer, and Kelley Tantau. 2020. "Coronavirus: Checkpoints catch Aucklanders fleeing for Coromandel baches." *Stuff*, August 12.

94 Menon, Praveen. 2020. "New Zealand considers freight as possible source of new coronavirus cluster." *Reuters*, August 11.

95 Tucker, Jeffrey A. 2020. "Is Immunity a Case of Rothbard's Lost Knowledge?" *American Institute for Economic Research*, August 2.

government in modern history.

New Zealand, a country of earnest people who pride themselves on intelligence and good government, took the theory of virus eradication through force to an extent not seen in any developed country. It went full barbarism, pitched by a suave politician with a charming accent. All was well. Now barbarism is back again. Look, I apologize for my sassy tone here. It's tragic what has happened to this wonderful country. It was my pleasure to visit there for a week. I, like many other Americans who visit, almost considered ripping up my return plane ticket. New Zealand looks and feels like paradise.

Sadly, thanks to brutal and deeply incompetent political leadership, that paradise is lost, lost to the superstitions of the Covid-19 faith that power, police, and adoring news coverage can scare a pathogen to go away and stay away. It might take a month, six months, or even a year, but it's coming. No amount of force will stop it.

Madness in Melbourne

Melbourne, that glorious city in the state of Victoria in Australia, granted me some of the best travel days of my life during two separate trips each lasting a full week. A happy, civilized, highly educated people are here living amidst modern architecture, inspiring bridges, and natural beauty, a place where even the police are kind, and when you ask them for directions they reply with a smile, and when you say thank you, they say "No worries."

Now there are big worries in Melbourne.

Australia is the only country in the world with a law that people can't be mean to each other. Now it is host to one of the world's meanest governments. The Premier has imposed a vicious police state without precedent in this country's history. His name is Dan Andrews (a sweet-sounding name that masks the tyrant he has become), and he tweets out pictures of empty streets to brag about what he has achieved in the name of suppressing a virus.[96] Tacitus's line about the Roman empire comes to mind: "Where they make a desert, they call it peace."

The catastrophe began with a spring lockdown before there were any cases of Covid-19, much less deaths. The ethos in Australia was one of extreme exclusion and suppression of the virus, not as bad as New Zealand but pretty bad. The rest of the world can catch this disease, but Australia would use its geographical isolation and political intelligence to ban the virus. The virus will be in awe and know to stay away forever. It's not a good theory because that's not how viruses work.

Still, it seemed to work, at first. That's because the virus had yet to

---

96 Andrews, Dan (@DanielAndrewsMP). 2020. "Thank you." *Twitter*, August 4.

arrive. When the virus did arrive, the futility of the suppression strategy was revealed. Melbourne had set up quarantine hotels for people arriving from abroad or returning from cruises. They would spend 14 days in isolation to purge themselves of possible infection. Then all would be okay. There was a problem: the wily virus escaped.[97]

As a result, a nation's pride in having suppressed the virus turned to panic and full lockdown. Internal borders are sealed. And Melbourne has become a living hell, not because of the virus (which is still mild) but because of the unleashing of a hellish police state, in which several thousand people living in nine public housing towers were placed under house arrest and unable to leave for ANY reason, with food rations delivered by the army, leading to appalling levels of personal trauma.[98] Then, the rest of Melbourne's five million residents were also put under lockdown. A friend summarized the situation across Melbourne for me:

- Police may now enter anyone's home **without a warrant**.
- Can't visit any family or friends.
- Can't go more than 3 miles from your home.[99]
- Curfew 8:00pm.
- $200 fine for no mask (mandatory masks at all times).
- $1,652 fine if outside without "a valid reason" – an amount being raised by the day[100]
- Can only exercise once per day, for up to 1 hour.
- Only one person per household, per day can leave the house (including for groceries).
- No gatherings of any size.

---

97 Thiessen, Tamara. 2020. "Australia: New Coronavirus Lockdown Melbourne Amid Sex, Lies, Quarantine Hotel Scandal." *Forbes*, July 7.

98 Yussuf, Ahmed. 2020. "The Aftermath of Melbourne's Housing Tower Lockdown: 'I Don't Know If I'm Ever Going to Be the Same Again.'" *SBS The Feed*, July 15.

99 Hurst, Daniel, and Josh Taylor. 2020. "Victoria announces stage four coronavirus lockdown restrictions including overnight curfew." *The Guardian*, August 2.

100 Christmass, Pip. 2020. "Victoria coronavirus fines handed out to 124 people in 24 hours for public health breaches." *7 News*, July 31.

- Weddings are illegal.
- Protests/activism is illegal; people have already been arrested for peaceful gatherings.
- Army is on the streets fining/arresting people.[101]
- 1984 dystopian language: billboards everywhere saying "Staying apart keeps us together."[102] Have they gone mad?
- "Since March 21, a total of 193,740 spot checks have been conducted by police across Victoria."
- Media is EXTREMELY biased, calls protesters "right wing conspiracy nutjobs" and won't allow discussion of whether these lockdowns are right or not.

Australia won't release the total amount of fines they've given out, but an ABC news report says it's over $5.2 million so far. Melbourne's streets are empty, even in a city of more than 5 million people. People are HATEFUL to each other, everyone is cannibalising their neighbours (calling police to report any little infraction of the rules and turning on each other like some socialist hellhole). They are prompted on by Victorian Premier Daniel Andrews who has shown complete and utter disdain for us, constantly blaming us. He's blamed children (yes, really) for not taking this seriously enough.

Every chance politicians get, they tell us it's *our* fault the virus is spreading (even though that's what viruses do – they spread). It's not just the Victorian Premier – the Australian Prime Minister Scott Morrison is just as terrible. He's encouraged all of this, and he was responsible for the first lockdown. To top it off there are billboards outside on the street that say in capital

101 Graham, Ben, and Phoebe Loomes. 2020. "Coronavirus Victoria: Anti-mask protesters arrested in Melbourne." *The Australian*, July 31.

102 QMS Media. 2020. "The Victorian Government dynamically updates their message on billboards across Victoria…" *Facebook*, May 1.

letters: "WHAT ARE YOU DOING? STAY HOME."[103] They feel extremely oppressive, like people are being yelled at by a very oppressive government. All because as of August 31, 2020, 565 people have died in the state of Victoria (total population is 6.359 million), where almost all of the deaths are over 70 with comorbidities, same as everywhere else in the world.[104]

This is lockdown ideology at work. It is tyranny without limit, at the expense of all human dignity, decency, and rights. The politicians make a desert and call it health. And yet, meanwhile, in Australia since March, there have been six times as many deaths from suicide than from Covid-19.[105] Like everywhere else on the planet, Melbourne will have to reach herd immunity from Covid-19 at some point. Those who deny that are risking not only liberty and health but civilization itself.

Perhaps the other states in Australia will observe the destruction in Victoria and learn to take another path when the virus first arrives in their territory, as it surely will. Lockdowns are not science; they are brutality. I cry for the once-great city of Melbourne today. May there be justice. And may its future political leadership be granted some modicum of decency and wisdom.

---

103 Eyewatch - Frankston Police Service Area. 2020. "Stay at home restrictions are now in place for Melbourne and Mitchell Shire…" *Facebook*, July 13.

104 Google. 2020. "Victoria Covid Deaths." *Google*.

105 Pratt, Rodney, and Jenny Ky. 2020. "Gus Worland talks mental health during COVID and the alarming rate of suicide in Australia." *The Morning Show*, August 6.

The History

The *New York Times* Revives
Its Grim Past

The resignation letter from former *New York Times* editor and writer Bari Weiss was so powerful because it seemed to state what many once-loyal readers – I was among them for many years, even given the obvious bias of the paper – already knew given the way things there have been going in the last year or so.[106] Something had gone very wrong at the newspaper of record. Weiss named it in a very satisfying letter writing with a burning desire to tell the truth.

> Op-eds that would have easily been published just two years ago would now get an editor or a writer in serious trouble, if not fired. If a piece is perceived as likely to inspire backlash internally or on social media, the editor or writer avoids pitching it. If she feels strongly enough to suggest it, she is quickly steered to safer ground. And if, every now and then, she succeeds in getting a piece published that does not explicitly promote progressive causes, it happens only after every line is carefully massaged, negotiated and caveated.

At this paper, dogma replaced reporting. Ideology displaced facts. All facts were filtered through an agenda. If something didn't fit the agenda, it was not reported. I had become so frustrated with this, especially during these lockdown months in which the paper seemed to have a rule of

---

106 Weiss, Bari. 2020. Resignation Letter. *BariWeiss.com*

blaming the virus and not the policy response for all existing problems, that I find it barely readable anymore. When precisely this happened is unclear. Some say that the "woke" generation had figured out how to troll the old-time liberals that used to run the shop. Some would name the 1619 Project, which might have been an interesting and important coming-to-terms with a dark side of American history but instead turned into a full-on trashing of every American value plus the existence of capitalism itself. (You can read Phil Magness's masterful response in book form.[107])

My own overwhelming consciousness that something had fallen apart began on February 27, 2020, with the *New York Times* podcast.[108] Reporter Donald McNeil told the host of this podcast that "this is alarmist, but I think right now, it's justified. This one reminds me of what I have read about the 1918 Spanish influenza."

Reminds him? That's his justification for spreading international panic? He claimed that "If you have 300 relatively close friends and acquaintances, six of them would die." The host of the show summed up McNeil's message: "2 percent lethality rate of 50 percent of the country," meaning 6.6 million dead. McNeil didn't disagree.

I was stunned because there was zero evidence for such outlandish claims. Not even Neil Ferguson predicted anything that ridiculous. Meanwhile, genuine experts were desperately trying to calm people down even as the *New York Times* was spreading maximum panic, probably for political reasons. In the weeks and months since then, the paper's Covid-19 doctrine has been set in stone. It goes like this. This is a terrifying pandemic. Many millions will die. Everyone is vulnerable. The only solution is to lock down. If we don't lock down, it is Trump's fault. Therefore Trump is responsible for all death. That message has been repeated thousands of times, every day in every way, ever since.

This is not science. It is not reporting. It is fanatical ideology in the guise of reporting. Thank goodness former *Times* reporters like Alex Berenson

---

107 Magness, Phillip W. 2020. *The 1619 Project: A Critique*. The American Institute for Economic Research: Massachusetts.

108 Barbaro, Michael, and Donald G. McNeil Jr. 2020. Podcast transcript: "The Coronavirus Goes Global." *The New York Times*, February 27.

continued to call them out daily.[109] Now, readers see all this and say to me: "Hey, things have never been right at this paper." I would dispute that. From 1934 to 1946, the great economic journalist Henry Hazlitt wrote not only a daily editorial but also curated the *Book Reviews*. There were times when the name Ludwig von Mises appeared on the front page of that review section, with glowing reviews of his books.

Even looking back at the paper's virus coverage of the postwar past, the rule was always the same: bring calm and urge trust of medical professionals to manage the disease but otherwise keep society functioning. That's what the paper said in 1957-58 (Asian Flu) and 1968-69 (Hong Kong Flu). The paper has a long tradition of trying to find that "vital center" while allowing editorials on either end of that so long as they seemed responsible. (As for its coverage during the Progressive Era, I'll leave that alone; it was nothing about which to brag.)

However, there is one gigantic, glaring, appalling, and essentially inexcusable exception to that. It is the case of Walter Duranty, the *Times's* bureau chief in Moscow from 1922 to 1936.[110] He was in a prime position to tell the truth about the catastrophic famines, political purges, rampant murders, and millions dead at the hands of the Soviet regime during those years. He was stationed there, ruled the roost, and had access to information denied to most of the rest of the world.

In particular, Duranty might have covered the millions who died (were slaughtered really) due to deliberate famine in Ukraine from 1932 to 1933. He did not. He did the opposite. In frequent articles for the *Times*, Duranty assured readers that all was well, that Stalin was a great leader, that everyone was more or less happy, that there was nothing to see in Ukraine. His later book was called *I Write as I Please* (1935). It should have been called *I Write to Please Stalin*. Incredibly, the paper won the Pulitzer Prize in 1932 for his coverage. The paper has never repudiated it. They still claim credit for it, despite the horrors that its pages were responsible

---

109 Berenson, Alex (@AlexBerenson). "1/ So let's be clear: long-haul #Covid is a joke…" *Twitter*, August 20.

110 Wikipedia. 2020. "Walter Duranty." *Wikipedia*, August 9.

for hiding from the world.

It's extremely difficult to face this terrible history but once you do, you experience a major example of how lies can perpetuate a killing machine. Duranty ruled the press in Moscow, suppressing truth in every way possible and convincing the world that all was well in the Soviet Union, even though it is quite clear from the documented history that he knew better. He preferred the lie to the truth, probably because he was being blackmailed but also because he was a communist and had absolutely no moral compass. To what extent his New York editors cooperated in this outrageous fraud remains unclear. At the very least, they wanted him to be correct so much that they didn't bother with an ounce of incredulity, even though he was exculpating and celebrating a totalitarian dictator.

It was this disgusting period of the paper's history that ultimately led to the cover-up of one of the century's greatest crimes. It was only revealed, through great moral courage, by journalist Malcolm Muggeridge (writing for the *Manchester Guardian*) and then by Gareth Jones, an independent English journalist who saw the suffering first hand, experienced near starvation, barely got out of Moscow, and, at great risk to himself and others, revealed the crimes of Stalin and the calamity in Ukraine to the world.[111] Which brings me to the real inspiration for this chapter: the 2019 movie Mr. Jones.[112] Which I urge you to watch. It's a riveting historical epic based entirely on the true story of Duranty, Orwell, and Jones.

Rarely has a movie haunted me so much. It's brilliant, mostly histori-cally accurate, and celebratory of the kind of moral courage it requires to cause truth to prevail over lies in an age of tyranny. How is it possible that millions could die and the world not know and so many people would cooperate in the deliberate suppression of truth – people who otherwise had prestige and privilege and reputations for integrity? It happens. It did happen. It will happen again, unless people are willing to stand up and say what is true. In some ways, it is happening now.

———————————

111 Wikipedia. 2020. "Gareth Jones (journalist)." *Wikipedia*, August 17.

112 Holland, Agnieszka. 2019. *Mr. Jones*. Film. Directed by Agnieszka Holland. Germany: Film Produkcja.

I'm pretty sure you know the feeling of looking at actual facts on the ground of this virus and then comparing them with the frenzied mania you get on the news daily, and especially at the *New York Times*, which only today (July 14, 2020) warned that countless others will die if we don't re-lockdown the entire country.[113]

It only takes a modicum of intelligence to realize that this writer is talking about "cases," which are overwhelmingly a result of required tests, mostly asymptomatic, and focused on the young and healthy who are in very little danger from this virus. We know this. We've known this since February. But he doesn't tell the readers that. Instead it is hysterical and urging more, more, more public panic and a national lockdown.

In these months, the pattern at the *Times* has been the same:

- Attribute terrible economic fallout not to the lockdowns but to the virus;
- Attribute virus fallout to the failure to lockdown enough;
- Deliberately confuse readers about the difference between tests, cases, and deaths;
- Never focus on the incredibly obvious demographics of Covid-19 death: average age 82 with underlying conditions;
- Ignore completely the primary victims of lockdowns: especially small businesses, the poor and minority groups, marginalized communities, artists, immigrant communities, small towns, small theaters, and so on.
- Do not publish anything that speaks of the path that all civilized countries prior dealt with new viruses: the vulnerable protect themselves while everyone else gets exposed with resulting immunity (Sweden did as well as any country because it refused to violate human rights);
- Dismiss any alternative to lockdown as crazy, unscientific, and cruel, while acting as if Fauci speaks for the whole of the scientific community;

---

113 Barry, John M. 2020. "The Pandemic Could Get Much, Much Worse. We Must Act Now." *The New York Times*, July 14.

- Above all, promote panic over calm.

From what I can tell, the last time that the *New York Times* ran anything realistic or sensible on this whole subject was March 20, 2020: Dr. David Katz on why the costs of lockdown are too high.[114] Re-reading it now, it is apparent that the editors forced him to dial back his views, because elsewhere he was much more explicit.

At this point, it's painful even to read their daily news reports, because they are all so transparently and obviously an extension of this above pattern and the larger agenda, which seems so obviously political. I don't believe that everyone at the *Times* approves of this; it's just an ethos that becomes self-enforcing in the interest of job retention and career ambition.

I've been asked countless times whether this censorship at the *Times* of serious commentary is driven by politics, and, namely, Trump hatred. As an early critic of the president and someone who has written probably several hundred articles criticizing many aspects of this administration's politics, the idea that an entire nation would be caused unthinkable suffering in the name of a holy war against Trump is basically unconscionable. Is it true? There is surely a grain of truth to the suspicions here, and even one grain is too much.

It is in this sense that the news reporting and editorial policies of the *New York Times* today reminds me of 1932 and the way in which journalism is being used to push out dogma over truth, selective facts over full and balanced coverage, ideology over tolerance, propaganda over diversity of opinion, and an aggressive political agenda over humane and careful journalism. It seems out of control at this point. This is why the inside testimony of Bari Weiss is so valuable and timely. Tolerance for different points of view sounds good in theory. In practice, there is an enormous draw toward righthink and the exercise of the cruelty toward those who land on the wrong side.

What can be done? In 1932, there weren't many alternatives to the *New York Times*. Today there are. It is up to each of us to get smart, get moral, sniff out and reject the lies, and find and tell the truth in other ways.

---

114 Katz, David L. 2020. "Is Our Fight Against Coronavirus Worse Than the Disease?" *The New York Times*, March 20.

The American Revolution Occurred in the Middle of a Pandemic

One of the most marvelous books I've read this year is Donald Henderson's personal story of the eradication of smallpox. The book is *Smallpox: The Death of a Disease - The Inside Story of Eradicating a Worldwide Killer*.[115] It's a brilliant and thrilling adventure story by a man who worked his entire life to make the world a better place. He was also the author (with others) of a mighty treatise against lockdowns that appears at AIER.[116] He died in 2016, which is tragic because we could have used his wisdom in these crazy times.

Smallpox is unknown to the current generation precisely because of Henderson's incredible work. It's a wicked disease. One in three who get it die.[117] Many are left with lifetime scars. It's horrid. In the entire centuries-old battle against it, however, no one ever imagined that lockdowns had anything to contribute to its management. What eradicated this horror was a serious effort on the part of medical professionals.

Smallpox was a huge player during the American Revolution. It was generally a greater threat to the troops than foreign armies. Every commanding officer had to deal with the problem. Many soldiers were so passionate about fighting that they inoculated themselves in secret and at

---

115 Henderson, Donald A., and Richard Preston. 2009. *Smallpox: The Death of a Disease: The Inside Story of Eradicating a Worldwide Killer*. Prometheus Books: Amherst, New York.

116 Stringham, Edward Peter. 2020. "How a Free Society Deals with Pandemics, According to Legendary Epidemiologist and Smallpox Eradicator Donald Henderson." *American Institute for Economic Research*, May 21.

117 Wikipedia. "Smallpox: Prognosis." *Wikipedia*, June 28.

great risk. Absolutely terrifying.

Here we are today (July 4, 2020) celebrating this Revolution while an entire nation cowers in fear of a virus that is hardly a threat at all to 99.5% of the population while the average age of death is two to four years longer than the average lifespan. There is not a single verified case of reinfection in the world, which implies that the immunities are easily acquired and sustained so far. For soldiers in the Revolutionary War, Covid-19 would have been hardly noticed. Instead they dealt with something far more ghastly. And yet they fought. For freedom.

Here is the story in brief from ArmyHeritage.org:

> During the Revolutionary War, one of the greatest threats to the Army came not from enemy bullets, but from disease. Perhaps the most dreaded disease was smallpox, caused by a virus that kills one out of every three infected people. Because smallpox was common in England, most British soldiers had already been exposed and were immune, but the disease was less common in America and the average Continental Soldier was not.
>
> As early as 1775, General George Washington knew smallpox was a serious problem for his Army. Throughout the fall and into the winter of 1775, an outbreak raged in the city of Boston. Rumors abounded that the British were deliberately spreading the disease. When the British finally evacuated Boston in March 1776, only Soldiers who had already had the disease were allowed into the city. Washington ordered his doctors to keep a sharp watch for smallpox and to send infected men to the isolation hospital immediately.
>
> Washington faced a difficult choice: whether or not to inoculate his Army. Inoculated soldiers would develop a mild case of the disease which most would survive. They would then be immune. His other option was to do nothing other than isolate and treat the sick and hope the Army avoided a major outbreak. There were three problems with inoculation. The first was that inoculated soldiers could transmit smallpox until fully recovered, so an inoculation program could trigger

an uncontrollable epidemic. Secondly, the inoculated soldiers would be unfit for duty for weeks while recovering, and as many as 2% of his soldiers could die. If the British attacked while the men were out of commission the Army could be destroyed. The third was that the inoculation process was simple enough that the men could do it themselves in secret.

Smallpox struck the Northern Army at Quebec, where many officers and men were secretly inoculating themselves, thus intensifying the epidemic. According to General Benedict Arnold, some 1,200 of the approximately 3,200 Continentals in the Montreal area were unfit for duty, most of them sick with smallpox. By the end of May 1776, the situation of Northern Department patients was "almost sufficient to excite the pity of Brutes, Large barns [being] filled with men at the very height of smallpox and not the least things, to make them comfortable and medicines being needed at both Fort George and Ticonderoga."

Smallpox threatened the destruction of the entire Army. Major General John Thomas, Commander of the Army in Quebec, died of smallpox. "The smallpox," mourned John Adams, "is ten times more terrible than Britons, Canadians and Indians, together." By mid-July 1776, an estimated three thousand men of the Northern Army were sick, most with smallpox. Eventually the epidemic eased and General Gates wrote to Washington that "the Smallpox is now perfectly removed from the Army." What exactly occurred has been lost to history, but sources suggest that the Northern Army proceeded with an inoculation program without authorization.

This was a risky move. Until mid-1776, the only authorized preventative measure was isolation of the sick. Inoculation was forbidden, though many soldiers secretly inoculated themselves. When Washington moved his Army to New York, he established a smallpox isolation hospital on an island in the East River and ordered a halt to all inoculations. The general warned that "any disobedience to this order will be most severely punished." The Continental Congress supported Washington, and when a private physician in the State of New York was caught inoculating soldiers he was jailed.

Despite these precautions, smallpox fear grew among the men of the Continental Army. Recruiting suffered, and by late June, official attitudes toward inoculation began to change. Despite precautions, the illness continued to spread. By August 1776, some troops were being inoculated in segregated camps.

Washington still feared triggering an epidemic, so he took careful precautions to ensure the isolation of soldiers undergoing inoculation, moving them out of Philadelphia and into nearby segregated hospitals. He suggested sheltering newly infected soldiers in houses in the remote countryside and urged that inoculated soldiers remain in isolation until fully recovered, and then issued either new or "well washed, air'd and smoaked" clothing. He recommended that the individual states immunize their recruits before sending them to join the Army.

In February 1777, while encamped at Morristown, Washington became convinced that only inoculation would prevent the destruction of his Army. Emphasizing the need for secrecy and speed, Washington ordered the inoculation of all troops. Because Virginia forbade inoculation, Washington asked Governor Patrick Henry to support the program, writing that smallpox "is more destructive to an Army in the Natural way, than the Enemy's Sword."

In the end, the gamble paid off. Fewer than 1% of the soldiers died from being inoculated, and the program was so successful in controlling smallpox that he repeated it in the Valley Forge winter of 1778.

How Global Capitalism
Boosted Immunities

From the beginning of this virus, political elites have used the language of war. The invisible enemy would be contained, suppressed, and beaten into submission. Then... it would retreat into the ether. The tactics would be travel bans, shutdowns, closures, mandatory human separation, and restrictions on breathing. The computer models proved it would work so surely it would – liberty, human rights, and freedom of association be damned.

We have all been used as non-player characters in a social experiment, untried in the whole history of humanity, and in ways that conflict with all values in which we previously believed as free societies.[118] No one in charge asked your opinion or mine. We are here merely to play our role in an agent-based model. It's the gamification of despotism.

The dogma has kept unfolding in ever stranger ways, such as with utterly contemptible restrictions on bars and restaurants, and even the claim that choirs, wind instruments, and the pipe organ itself spreads disease.[119] The American Guild of Organists has been forced to provide a long document justifying the existence of church music.[120] The devastation

---

118 Wikipedia. 2020. "Non-player character." *Wikipedia*, June 2.

119 Thierer, Adam. 2020. "Ridiculous Liquor Regulations." *American Institute for Economic Research*, July 25.

120 AGO. 2020. "COVID-19 and Organists: Q & A." *American Guild of Organists*, July 17.

in the arts community is palpable.[121] The carnage is truly unfathomable. And getting worse: regulations on elevators will make America's mighty skyscrapers unusable and pointless.

What if the entire paradigm is wrong? No book on cell and molecular biology that I've found mentions lockdowns and hiding as ways to beat a virus. "For most viruses that attack humans," says *Cell and Molecular Biology for Dummies*, "your only defenses are prevention and your own immune systems."[122] Strange isn't it? Nothing about the awesome power of politicians to crush a virus. It should come as no surprise that the most comprehensive and global statistical analysis yet conducted concludes that "rapid border closures, full lockdowns, and wide-spread testing were not associated with Covid-19 mortality per million people" – which to say there is no evidence that any of this ghastly destruction saved lives.[123]

A strikingly odd feature of media rhetoric during these terrible months has been the silencing of voices that speak of immunity as the way to defeat a virus of this sort. AIER has reported them when they appear but, as a seriously disgruntled reader of the *New York Times*, I can tell you that immunities via antibodies have not made their coverage much at all. In a way that stuns me, this has suddenly changed with a coherent write up that appeared yesterday: "Can You Get Covid-19 Again? It's Very Unlikely, Experts Say."[124] This accurate piece amounts to a refutation of one of thousands of ridiculous popular articles claiming that this virus is so unprecedented, so lethal, so mysterious, that the only option is to throw out all morality and treat people like animals. Says the *Times*:

---

121 Tucker, Jeffrey A. 2020. "The Lockdowns Are Killing the Arts." *American Institute for Economic Research*, July 14.

122 Kratz, Rene Fester. 2009. *Molecular & Cell Biology For Dummies*. John Wiley & Sons: Hoboken, New Jersey.

123 Chaudhry, Rabail, George Dranitsaris, Talha Mubashir, Justyna Bartoszko, Sheila Riazi. 2020. "A country level analysis measuring the impact of government actions, country preparedness and socioeconomic factors on COVID-19 mortality and related health outcomes." *EClinicalMedicine*, July 21.

124 Mandavilli, Apoorva. 2020. "Can You Get Covid-19 Again? It's Very Unlikely, Experts Say." *The New York Times*, July 22.

While little is definitively known about the coronavirus, just seven months into the pandemic, the new virus is behaving like most others… It may be possible for the coronavirus to strike the same person twice, but it's highly unlikely that it would do so in such a short window or to make people sicker the second time, they said… **People infected with the coronavirus typically produce immune molecules called antibodies.** Several teams have recently reported that the levels of these antibodies decline in two to three months, causing some consternation.[125] But a drop in antibodies is perfectly normal after an acute infection subsides, said Dr. Michael Mina, an immunologist at Harvard University. Many clinicians are "scratching their heads saying, 'What an extraordinarily odd virus that it's not leading to robust immunity,' but they're totally wrong," Dr. Mina said. "It doesn't get more textbook than this."

Imagine that: "immune molecules called antibodies." The *Times* writes as if it is introducing a new vocabulary word here, even though George Washington's troops understood the point and dangerously pursued inoculation techniques against smallpox.[126] So let us think about this. You get the Covid-19 virus, you get over it (as 99.6% do, especially healthy people) and then you gain protection against that virus and possibly other similar viruses for a time. Your immune system improves. The million-year coevolution of humans and viruses takes another step in the direction of progress. The implication: rather than run and hide, maybe a bit of scientifically informed bravery is in order here.

---

125 Lei, Qing, Yang Li, Hongyan Hou, Feng Wang, Yandi Zhang, et al. 2020. "Antibody dynamics to SARS-CoV-2 in asymptomatic COVID-19 infections." *MedRxiv*, August 4; Long, Quan-Xin, Xiao-Jun Tang, Qiu-Lin Shi, Qin Li, Hai-Jun Deng, et al. 2020. "Clinical and immunological assessment of asymptomatic SARS-CoV-2 infections." *Nature Medicine*, 26: 1200-1204.

126 Tucker, Jeffrey A. 2020. "The American Revolution Occurred in the Middle of a Pandemic." *The American Institute for Economic Research*, July 4.

Yes, but if true, wouldn't competent and credentialled epidemiologists be saying this? It turns out that many are. They just aren't getting a hearing because the media and politicians ignore them. One of the brave and intelligent voices here is Sunetra Gupta, the professor of theoretical epidemiology who leads a full team of experts at Oxford University. Her understanding is so profound that she has, in an interview, offered up a fascinating thesis concerning why the flu pandemic of 1918 was the last truly catastrophic plague we've seen in the modern world.[127]

Gupta's claim is that when we live in isolated tribes that are sheltered from exposure, those people gradually become weaker and more vulnerable. The wrong pathogen arrives at the wrong time and the people have not been biologically prepared for it. It wipes them out in shocking ways. But with modern capitalism came the end of such sterile isolation. It gave us new methods of travelling, mixing, associating, moving, and consequently led to more exposure to disease and the resulting antibodies. Hence, it is not just better therapeutics and vaccines that helped us conquer some plagues but immunities themselves. Our biological toolkit for fighting disease became improved simply through travel, trade, and global commerce.

I quote Gupta at length, beginning with her tutorial on virus immunity 101 gained over the course of last century and oddly forgotten in this century:

> The other interesting issue that I've suddenly realised with this particular threat, is that people are treating it like an external disaster, like a hurricane or a tsunami, as if you can batten down the hatches and it will be gone eventually. **That is simply not correct.** The epidemic is an ecological relationship that we have to manage between ourselves and the virus. But instead, people are looking at it as a completely external thing…. That's the axis of disease, but then there's the socioeconomic axis, which has been ignored. But there's a third, aesthetic access, which is about how we want to live our lives. **We are closing ourselves off not just to the disease, but to other aspects of being human…**

---

127 Reaction. 2020. "We may already have herd immunity – an interview with Professor Sunetra Gupta." *Reaction*, July 21.

I think the trade-off is very extreme. Obviously the most extreme manifestation of that trade-off is the 23 million people who will be pushed below the poverty line as a result of this sledgehammer approach. The costs to the arts is I think also incredibly profound – the theatres and all other forms of performing art. But also the inherent art of living, which I think is being compromised.

Acts of kindness are being eschewed. Someone was telling me yesterday that their mother said to them "please don't come home, you're going to kill us"…

Now I see young people being terrified, even though they realise the risk to themselves is low, that they might infect a friend who will then give it to their grandparents. This chain of guilt is somehow located on the individual rather than being distributed and shared.

We have to share the guilt. We have to share the responsibility. And we have to take on board certain risks ourselves in order to fulfil our obligations and to uphold the social contract. So I'd like the politicians to remind people of that, because that's what they've been elected to do – to see the social contract is being properly transacted…

It's very difficult. I think there's nothing to do except remind people that that is not only puritanical, but misguided. Because actually, **the only way we can reduce the risk to the vulnerable people in the population is, for those of us who are able to acquire herd immunity, to do that.**

Even if there is a little bit of a risk. I'm 55 years old, there's some slight risk out there. But I would be willing to take that, just as I do with the flu. There's a risk I might die of flu, but I'm willing to take that risk, because I know that if I don't then flu will appear as it did before, it will enter the population of immunologically naive individuals, and then there will be a high risk of infection which will have a **disproportionate effect on the vulnerable sector of the population.**

Maybe the way to counter it now is to say, actually, **not only**

is it a good thing for young people to go out there and become immune, but that is almost their duty. It's a way of living with this virus. It's how we live with other viruses. Flu is clearly a very dangerous virus, but the reason we don't see more deaths from flu every year is because, through herd immunity, the levels of infection are kept to as low a level as we can get...

Now to more on the beautiful seeming magic of herd immunity, which has most recently been estimated to be 10-20%:[128]

[Herd immunity is] a technical term for the proportion of the population that needs to be immune in order to prevent the disease from spreading, which is the central concept in vaccinations. It's a fundamental epidemiological concept, which clearly has been subverted. I guess the fact it includes the word herd has made it easier.

The truth is that **herd immunity is a way of preventing vulnerable people from dying.** It is achieved at the expense of some people dying, and we can stop that by protecting the vulnerable class in the process. In an ideal situation, you would protect the vulnerable as best you can, let people go about their business, allow herd immunity to build up, make sure the economy doesn't crash, make sure the arts are preserved, and make sure qualities of kindness and tolerance remain in place.

We live, it seems, in this state of terror. Yes, international travel facilitates the entrance of contagion, but what it also does is it brings immunity.

And finally to the implications for history and the way global capitalism both ended our sterile isolation but also brought us biological immunity and longer lives.

---

128 Aguas, Ricardo, Rodrigo M. Corder, Jessica G. King, Guilherme Goncalves, Marcelo U. Ferreira, et al. 2020. "Herd immunity thresholds for SARS-CoV-2 estimated from unfolding epidemics." *MedRxiv*, July 24.

Why don't we get flu pandemics anymore? Because before 1918 there was not sufficient international travel or densities of individuals to keep flu on as the sort of seasonal thing it is now. Pockets of non-immune people would build up, and then they would be ravaged.

That was the pattern until the end of the First World War. Since then, many of these diseases have become endemic. As a result of which we are much more exposed to diseases in general and related pathogens, so if something new comes along we are much better off than we would be if we hadn't had some sort of exposure to it.

If coronavirus had arrived in a setting where we had no coronavirus exposure before, we might be much worse off. It also seems that in addition to protection against severe disease as a result of exposure to related coronaviruses, some fraction of us seem to be resistant to infection.

That's just fantastic news, actually. Hopefully that will be consolidated at a scientific, laboratory level. We ourselves are looking at how antibodies to seasonal coronaviruses can impact on protection against infection and disease.

Maybe we will be able to build up a picture that will reassure the public that actually we are much better off having been exposed to related coronaviruses. We are in a better place to fight off this infection than we actually thought.

One might think that this learned professor's outlook, offered from her position at perhaps the world's most prestigious university, would hold some sway over media and politics. The implications of what she says are not only that the lockdowns are wrong. Not only that the closures are pointless. She goes further: they are making us less healthy, and taking steps to revert the progress of health we have made over a century of travel, mixing, and close commercial relationships.

The implications of Gupta's view – and its flipping of the run-and-hide, shelter-in-place narrative – offer a promising new way to understand the relationship between modern capitalism and the dramatic improve-ments in human health we've experienced over a century. It also sends up a warning flare: if we stay on the present course of hiding and futilely trying to suppress the virus, we will end up making all of society poorer both materially and spiritually and also delivering a dangerous blow to our biological health.

The 2006 Origins of the
Lockdown Idea

I n the Spring of 2020 began the grand effort, on display in thousands of articles and news broadcasts daily, somehow to normalize the lockdown and all its destruction. We didn't lock down almost the entire country in 1968/69, 1957, or 1949-1952, or even during 1918.[129] But in a terrifying few days in March 2020, it happened to all of us, causing an avalanche of social, cultural, and economic destruction that will ring through the ages.

There was nothing normal about it all. We will be trying to figure out what happened to us for decades hence. How did a temporary plan to preserve hospital capacity turn into two-to-three months of near-universal house arrest that ended up causing worker furloughs at 256 hospitals, cessation of international travel, 40% job losses among people earning less than $40K per year, devastation of every economic sector, mass confusion and demoralization, the complete disregard of all fundamental rights and liberties, not to mention the mass confiscation of private property with forced closures of millions of businesses?[130]

What's truly surprising is just how recent the theory behind lockdown

---

129 Tucker, Jeffrey A. 2020. "Woodstock Occurred in the Middle of a Pandemic." *American Institute for Economic Research*, May 1; Tucker, Jeffrey A. 2020. "Elvis Was King, Ike Was President, and 116,000 Americans Died in a Pandemic." *American Institute for Economic Research*, May 4; Tucker, Jeffrey A. 2020. "No Lockdowns: The Terrifying Polio Pandemic of 1949-52." *American Institute for Economic Research*, May 10; Geloso, Vincent. 2020. "Spanish Flu Was Awful But We Moved On Anyway." *American Institute for Economic Research*, April 14.

130 Paavola, Alia. 2020. "266 hospitals furloughing workers in response to COVID-19." *Becker's Hospital Review*, April 7; Tucker, Jeffrey A. 2020. "'I've Lost Faith in Humanity': The Psychological Toll of the Lockdown." *American Institute for Economic Research*, April 28.

and forced distancing actually is. So far as anyone can tell, the intellectual machinery that made this mess was invented 14 years ago, and not by epidemiologists but by computer-simulation modelers. It was adopted not by experienced doctors—they warned ferociously against it—but by politicians.

Let's start with the phrase "social distancing," which has mutated into forced human separation. The first I had heard it was in the 2011 movie *Contagion*. The first time it appeared in the *New York Times* was February 12, 2006:[131]

> If the avian flu goes pandemic while Tamiflu and vaccines are still in short supply, experts say, the only protection most Americans will have is "social distancing," which is the **new politically correct way of saying "quarantine."**
>
> But distancing also encompasses less drastic measures, like wearing face masks, staying out of elevators—and the [elbow] bump. Such stratagems, those experts say, will rewrite the ways we interact, at least during the weeks when the waves of influenza are washing over us.

Maybe you don't remember that the avian flu of 2006 didn't amount to much. It's true, despite all the extreme warnings about its lethality, H5N1 didn't turn into much at all.[132] What it did do, however, was send the existing president, George W. Bush, to the library to read about the 1918 flu and its catastrophic results. He asked for some experts to submit some plans to him about what to do when the real thing comes along. The *New York Times* tells the story from there:[133]

---

131 McNeil, Donald G. Jr. 2006. "Greetings Kill: Primer for a Pandemic." *The New York Times*, February 12.

132 CDC. 2018. "Highly Pathogenic Asian Avian Influenza A(H5N1) Virus." *CDC*, December 12.

133 Lipton, Eric, and Jennifer Steinhauer. 2020. "The Untold Story of the Birth of Social Distancing." *The New York Times*, April 22.

Fourteen years ago, two federal government doctors, Richard Hatchett and Carter Mecher, met with a colleague at a burger joint in suburban Washington for a final review of a proposal they knew would be treated like a piñata: telling Americans to stay home from work and school the next time the country was hit by a deadly pandemic.

When they presented their plan not long after, it was met with skepticism and a degree of ridicule by senior officials, who like others in the United States had grown accustomed to relying on the pharmaceutical industry, with its ever-growing array of new treatments, to confront evolving health challenges.

Drs. Hatchett and Mecher were proposing instead that Americans in some places might have to turn back to an approach, self-isolation, first widely employed in the Middle Ages.

How that idea—born out of a request by President George W. Bush to ensure the nation was better prepared for the next contagious disease outbreak—**became the heart of the national playbook for responding to a pandemic** is one of the untold stories of the coronavirus crisis.

It required the key proponents—Dr. Mecher, a Department of Veterans Affairs physician, and Dr. Hatchett, an oncologist turned White House adviser—to overcome intense initial opposition.

It brought their work together with that of a Defense Department team assigned to a similar task.

And it had some unexpected detours, including a deep dive into the history of the 1918 Spanish flu and an important discovery **kicked off by a high school research project pursued by the daughter of a scientist** at the Sandia National Laboratories.

The concept of social distancing is now intimately familiar to almost everyone. But as it first made its way through the federal bureaucracy in 2006 and 2007, it was viewed as **impractical, unnecessary and politically infeasible.**

Notice that in the course of this planning, neither legal nor economic experts were brought in to consult and advise. Instead it fell to Mecher (formerly of Chicago and an intensive care doctor with no previous expertise in pandemics) and the oncologist Hatchett. But what is this mention of the high-school daughter of 14? Her name is Laura M. Glass,[134] and she recently declined to be interviewed when the *Albuquerque Journal* did a deep dive of this history.[135]

> Laura, with some guidance from her dad, devised a computer simulation that showed how people—family members, co-workers, students in schools, people in social situations—interact. What she discovered was that school kids come in contact with about 140 people a day, more than any other group. Based on that finding, her program showed that in a hypothetical town of 10,000 people, 5,000 would be infected during a pandemic if no measures were taken, but only 500 would be infected if the schools were closed.

Laura's name appears on the foundational paper arguing for lockdowns and forced human separation. That paper is "Targeted Social Distancing Designs for Pandemic Influenza" (2006).[136] It set out a model for forced separation and applied it with good results backwards in time to 1957. They conclude with a chilling call for what amounts to a totalitarian lockdown, all stated very matter-of-factly.

> Implementation of social distancing strategies is challenging. They likely must be imposed for the duration of the local epidemic and possibly until a strain-specific vaccine is developed and distributed. If **compliance with the strategy is high** over this period, an epidemic within a community can be averted.

----

134 A previous version of this article in one instance incorrectly named the coauthor of the 2006 paper by Robert Glass. That is now corrected to Laura M. Glass.

135 Reed, Ollie Jr. 2020. "Social distancing born in ABQ teen's science project." *Albuquerque Journal*, May 2.

136 Glass, Robert J., Laura M. Glass, Walter E. Beyeler, and H. Jason Min. 2006. "Targeted Social Distancing Designs for Pandemic Influenza." *CDC Emerging Infectious Diseases*, 12(11).

However, if neighboring communities do not also use these interventions, infected neighbors will continue to introduce influenza and prolong the local epidemic, albeit at a depressed level more easily accommodated by healthcare systems.

In other words, it was a high-school science experiment that eventually became law of the land, and through a circuitous route propelled not by science but politics. The primary author of this paper was Robert J. Glass, a complex-systems analyst with Sandia National Laboratories. He had no medical training, much less an expertise in immunology or epidemiology. That explains why Dr. D.A. Henderson, "who had been the leader of the international effort to eradicate smallpox," completely rejected the whole scheme. Says the *NYT*:

Dr. Henderson was convinced that it made no sense to force schools to close or public gatherings to stop. Teenagers would escape their homes to hang out at the mall. School lunch programs would close, and impoverished children would not have enough to eat. Hospital staff would have a hard time going to work if their children were at home.

The measures embraced by Drs. Mecher and Hatchett would "result in significant disruption of the social functioning of communities and result in possibly serious economic problems," Dr. Henderson wrote in his own academic paper responding to their ideas.

The answer, he insisted, was to tough it out: **Let the pandemic spread, treat people who get sick and work quickly to develop a vaccine to prevent it from coming back.**

AIER's Phil Magness got to work to find the literature responding to the 2006 paper by Robert and Laura M. Glass and discovered the following manifesto: "Disease Mitigation Measures in the Control of Pandemic Influenza."[137] The authors included D.A. Henderson, along with three

---

137 Glass et al. (2006); Stringham (2020,"How a Free Society Deals with Pandemics...").

professors from Johns Hopkins: infectious disease specialist Thomas V. Inglesby, epidemiologist Jennifer B. Nuzzo, and physician Tara O'Toole. Their paper is a remarkably readable refutation of the entire lock-down model.[138] Their remarkable conclusion?

> Experience has shown that communities faced with epidemics or other adverse events respond best and with the least anxiety when the **normal social functioning of the community is least disrupted.** Strong political and public health leadership to provide reassurance and to ensure that needed medical care services are provided are critical elements. If either is seen to be less than optimal, **a manageable epidemic could move toward catastrophe.**

Confronting a manageable epidemic and turning it into a catastrophe: that seems like a good description of everything that has happened in the Covid-19 crisis of 2020.

Thus did some of the most highly trained and experienced experts on epidemics warn with biting rhetoric against everything that the advocates of lockdown proposed. It was not even a real-world idea in the first place and showed no actual knowledge of viruses and disease mitigation. Again, the idea was born of a high-school science experiment using agent-based modelling techniques having nothing at all to do with real life, real science, or real medicine. So the question becomes: how did the extreme view prevail?

The *New York Times* has the answer:[139]

> The [Bush] administration ultimately sided with the proponents of social distancing and shutdowns—though their victory was little noticed outside of public health circles. Their policy would become the basis for government planning and would be used extensively in simulations used to prepare for pandemics, and

---

138 Stringham (2020, "How a Free Society Deals with Pandemics…").

139 Lipton and Steinhauer (2020).

in a limited way in 2009 during an outbreak of the influenza called H1N1.[140] **Then the coronavirus came, and the plan was put to work across the country for the first time.[141]**

The *Times* called one of the pro-lockdown researchers, Dr. Howard Markel, and asked what he thought of the lockdowns. His answer: he is glad that his work was used to "save lives" but added, **"It is also horrifying."** "We always knew this would be applied in worst-case scenarios," he said. "Even when you are working on dystopian concepts, you always hope it will never be used."

Ideas have consequences, as they say. Dream up an idea for a virus-controlling totalitarian society, one without an endgame and eschewing any experienced-based evidence that it would achieve the goal, and you might see it implemented someday. Lockdown might be the new orthodoxy but that doesn't make it medically sound or morally correct. At least now we know that many great doctors and scholars in 2006 did their best to stop this nightmare from unfolding. Their mighty paper should serve as a blueprint for dealing with the next pandemic.

---

140 Navarro, J. Alexander, Katrin S. Kohl, Martin S. Cetron, and Howard Markel. 2016. "A Tale of Many Cities: A Contemporary Historical Study of the Implementation of School Closures during the 2009 pA(H1N1) Influenza Pandemic." *Journal of health politics, policy and law,* 41(3), 393–421.

141 See: CDC. 2020. *Interim Pre-pandemic Planning Guidance: Community Strategy for Pandemic Influenza Mitigation in the United States—Early, Targeted, Layered Use of Nonpharmaceutical Interventions.* Centres for Disease Control and Prevention (CDC), February. It is arguable that this paper did not favor full lockdown. I've spoken to Rajeev Venkayya, MD, who regards the 2007 plan as more liberal, and assures me that they never envisioned this level of lockdown: "Lockdowns and shelter-in-place were not part of the recommendations." To my mind, fleshing out the full relationship between this 2007 document and current policy requires a separate article.

The 2007 Origins of Forced School Closings and Mandatory Human Separation

The idea of a full lockdown of society in the event of a pandemic first emerged as an extremist proposal in 2006, issued by a computer scientist as part of George W. Bush's preparations for biowarfare. It provoked a fierce response by the world's leading epidemiologist Donald Henderson and his colleagues.[142] That proposal, issued by Robert Glass under the influence of his daughter's high school science fair project (yes, it thanks Neil Ferguson for comments), would sit for 14 years before being deployed in some form during the political panic of March 2020.[143]

The blueprint document – more moderate than the Glass paper but still draconian – that sat lying in wait in the intervening years was issued in February 2007: "Interim Pre-pandemic Planning Guidance: Community Strategy for Pandemic Influenza Mitigation in the United States— Early, Targeted, Layered Use of Nonpharmaceutical Interventions."[144] This document introduced the new lexicon: Targeted Layered Containment (TLC), Non-Pharmaceutical Interventions (NPIs), Social Distancing, Flatten the Curve. By the middle of March 2020, all of these strange phrases were on the lips of every news broadcaster and politician.

---

142 Stringham, Edward Peter. 2020. "How a Free Society Deals with Pandemics, According to Legendary Epidemiologist and Smallpox Eradicator Donald Henderson." *American Institute for Economic Research*, May 21.

143 Stringham, Edward Peter. 2020. "Was Lockdown Architect and Theoretical Physicist Neil Ferguson Morally Right To Defy the Lockdown?" *American Institute for Economic Research*, May 18.

144 CDC (2007, *Interim Pre-pandemic Planning Guidance:....*).

It was new vocabulary for new times which rejected the non-government solutions used in every pandemic since World War II. Hereafter, government would be hands-on with precision policies that infringe on liberties and property, with the presumption that under emergency conditions, government can do essentially anything that it wants.

The document did not push a hard lockdown but it did call for closures of all schools and large events, in addition to:

> **Voluntary** home quarantine of members of households with confirmed or probable influenza case(s) and consideration of combining this intervention with the prophylactic use of antiviral medications, providing sufficient quantities of effective medications exist and that a feasible means of distributing them is in place.

On its face, there is nothing inherently threatening about a voluntary home quarantine of the sick. All of this happens in any case, normally and naturally, in all seasons in which viruses and bacteria threaten health, which is to say always. It requires no governing directives. There is no reason for government to weigh in on the matter at all. However, matters are different with other directives from this 2007 document, including:

> * Dismissal of students from school (including public and private schools as well as colleges and universities) and school-based activities and closure of childcare programs, coupled with protecting children and teenagers through social distancing in the community to achieve reductions of out-of-school social contacts and community mixing.

> * Use of social distancing measures to reduce contact between adults in the community and workplace, including, for example, cancellation of large public gatherings and alteration of workplace environments and schedules to decrease social density and preserve a healthy workplace to the greatest extent possible without disrupting essential services. Enable institution of workplace

leave policies that align incentives and facilitate adherence with the nonpharmaceutical interventions (NPIs) outlined above.

While these measures might seem moderate by comparison to what happened in March 2020, these directives arguably led to lockdown just by the logic of intervention and the general theory that viruses should be defeated by overriding private decision-making and forced human separation.

In a market-based free society, everything is connected and one closure leads to another. Dismiss the schools and the kids hang out in malls, beaches, and parks. You have to close them to maintain distancing. If they stay home, they need a parent home, which puts pressure on businesses to close. If you are closing "large public gatherings" you still have a problem with churches, picnics, conventions of any size, and even large dinner parties. Transportation has to shut down, including flights, trains, and subways. A consistent application of the logic here – that the way to mitigate disease is to stay away from people – requires a complete shutdown of society.

And to what end? Epidemiologists will tell you that viruses don't just get bored and go away. Natural immunity requires the building of antibodies to the virus. Then there is the option of vaccines, which have historically been long in the discovery, distribution, and administration. The first smallpox vaccine appeared in 1796; the disease wasn't declared eradicated until 1980.[145] But to the authors of the 2007 CDC directive, vaccines are the end game, even without evidence that they are possible in the case of new viruses such as Covid-19.

The point of closures, said the CDC, is to "delay the exponential growth in incident cases and shift the epidemic curve to the right in order to 'buy time' for production and distribution of a well-matched pandemic strain vaccine."

To be sure, back in 2006 and 2007, there were plenty of serious protests against this whole line of thinking. Some experts called it disruptive,

---

145 Stringham, Edward Peter. 2020. "Stand Up for Your Rights, says Bio-Statistician Knut M. Wittkowski." *American Institute for Economic Research*, April 6.

dangerous, and potentially calamitous, and pushed instead the old wisdom we had learned after World War II: disease mitigation efforts should be handled by medical professionals, not politicians. When the 1957-58 Asian flu broke out (eventually killing 116,000 Americans), for example, the *New York Times* expressed the common wisdom: "Let us all keep a cool head about Asian influenza as the statistics on the spread and the virulence of the disease begin to accumulate."[146] That was the one editorial the paper ran on the topic. It was the opposite of a media frenzy.

Lockdowns, as well as all this language and apparatus that amount to a primal scream to run and hide from the virus, were once considered bad law and bad medicine, and thus completely out of the question. The general rule was to stay calm, get immunities, and move forward with life without disruption. And that is where matters stood all these years, just waiting to be deployed by a handful of guardians of the strategy to undertake a great experiment in massive public control. Beginning in January of this year, as news of Covid-19 was pouring out of Wuhan, China, many of those who were involved in crafting this policy in 2007 began to sense an opportunity. As the *New York Times* explains:[147]

> As the coronavirus emerged and headed toward the United States, an extraordinary conversation was hatched among an elite group of infectious disease doctors and medical experts in the federal government and academic institutions around the nation.
>
> Red Dawn — a nod to the 1984 film with Patrick Swayze and Charlie Sheen — was the nickname for the email chain they built. Different threads in the chain were named Red Dawn Breaking, Red Dawn Rising, Red Dawn Breaking Bad and, as the situation grew more dire, Red Dawn Raging. It was hosted by the chief medical officer at the Department of Homeland Security, Dr. Duane C. Caneva, starting in January

---

146 1957. Editorial. *The New York Times*, September 17.

147 Lipton, Eric. 2020. "The 'Red Dawn' Emails: 8 Key Exchanges on the Faltering Response to the Coronavirus." *The New York Times*, April 11.

with a small core of medical experts and friends that gradually grew to dozens.

One of the most active participants on this thread was Carter Mecher, a Chicago physician who has long worked for the Veterans Administration as an advisor. He was actively involved in crafting the 2007 CDC document on school shutdowns and forced human separation. Mecher had been a convert to the ideas of Robert and Laura Glass and their blueprint for full lockdown.[148] With the Glass father and daughter out of the picture, it was left to Mecher to push hard for a new approach to handling viruses. He more than anyone in the email thread posted often and with rising passion. On January 28, 2020, he sent the following note:

> **From: Carter Mecher**
> **Sent: 28 Jan 2020, at 18:04**
> The chatter on the blogs is that WHO and CDC are behind the curve. I'm seeing comments from people asking why WHO and CDC seem to be downplaying this. I'm certainly no public health expert (just a dufus from the VA), but no matter how I look at this, it looks be bad. If we assume the same case ascertainment rate as the spring wave of 2009 H1N1, this looks nearly as transmissible as flu (but with a longer incubation period and greater Ro). The projected size of the outbreak already seems hard to believe

The following month, he was already talking up Non-Pharmaceutical Interventions, a broad phrase that can mean everything from voluntary self-quarantine all the way to full lockdown.

> **From: Carter Mecher**
> **Sent: Monday, February 17, 2020 8:57 AM**
> NPIs are going to be central to our response to this outbreak (assuming our estimates of severity prove accurate). This email group has grown since we began (not quite epidemic-level growth, but getting there). Looking ahead, I anticipate we might encounter pushback over the implementation of NPIs and would expect similar concerns/arguments as were raised back in 2006 when this strategy first emerged.

---

148 Glass, Robert J., Laura M. Glass, Walter E. Beyeler, and H. Jason Min. 2006. "Targeted Social Distancing Designs for Pandemic Influenza." *Emerging Infectious Diseases,* 12(11):1671-1681.

The same day, Mecher began to promote the pro-lockdown work of Robert Glass:[149]

> Lastly, another person, Bob Glass at Los Alamos, also did work on this separately from the MIDAS group. He actually began this work as part of a science fair project for his daughter (using social contacts of his daughter and her classmates at school to model disease transmission). He knew someone at VA who forwarded his work to us (chain of transmission). Early on (even before the MIDAS group modeled TLC), we had a Eureka moment when we graphed his data in Excel (can share that single graph to anyone interested).

After this, the tone and tenor of the group grew ever more fiery to the point of absolute frenzy. They needed the disease threat as intense as possible in order to kick off their plans, and they were probably sincere in believing it was time. As with any long email chain, there eventually emerges one tone setting and driver of discussion. In this case, Mecher became the main voice for panic and immediate deployment of the shutting of schools and public events, leading to lockdowns all over the country.

If you have any doubt that the main push for the lockdown was less about therapy than models, inspired by the fantasies of a computer scientist rather than a genuine expert in viruses, a social experiment conducted with disregard for freedom and the rule of law, a wild and foolhardy central plan hatched without regard to experience or serious medical science, this email chain as passionate demand to implement the 2007 CDC blueprint is the proof.

Now the architects of 2007 are working themselves to socially distance from the lockdowns that have wrought so much damage to the country. I'm not so sure if they can or deserve to be declared free of responsibility. How many terrible atrocities in wartime result from a policy that began

149 Full 'Red Dawn' Email Chain available from: Lipton, Eric. 2020. "The 'Red Dawn' Emails: 8 Key Exchanges on the Faltering Response to the Coronavirus." *The New York Times*, April 11.

with a promise of only surgical strikes and precision bombings with no other casualties? We see something similar taking place here. Culpability belongs to those who unleash violence in the name of peace, or health.

The Terrifying Polio
Pandemic of 1949-52

World War II had ended four years earlier and the US was trying to return to peace and prosperity. Price controls and rationing were ended. Trade was opening. People were returning to normal life. The economy started humming again. Optimism for the future was growing. Harry Truman became the symbol of a new normacy. From Depression and war, society was on the mend.

As if to serve as a reminder that there were still threats to life and liberty present, an old enemy made its appearance: polio. It's a disease with ancient origins, with its most terrifying effect, the paralysis of the lower extremities. It maimed children, killed adults, and struck enormous fear into everyone. Polio is also a paradigmatic case in point that targeted and localized policy mitigations have worked in the past, but society-wide lockdowns had never been used prior to Covid-19. They weren't even considered an option.

Polio was not an unknown disease: its reputation for cruelty was well-earned. In the 1916 outbreak, there were 27,000 cases and more than 6,000 deaths due to polio in the United States, 2,000 of which were in New York City. After the war, people had living memories of this horror. People were also used to adjusting their behavior. In 1918, people left cities for resorts, movie theaters were closed for lack of customers, groups cancelled meetings, and public gatherings dwindled. Children avoided swimming pools and public water fountains, fearing that it was transmitted through water. Whatever the therapeutic merit of this, these actions required no force; it happened because people did their best to adapt to risk and be cautious.

In 1949, the new polio epidemic appeared and swept through selective population centers, leaving its most tragic sign: children with wheelchairs, crutches, leg braces, and deformed limbs. For children with polio in the late 1940s, the disease caused paralysis in 1 in 1,000 cases of children aged 5 to 9. The rest had only mild symptoms and developed immunities. In the 1952 season, of the 57,628 cases reported, 3,145 died and a shocking 21,269 experienced paralysis. So while the infection, death, and paralysis rates seem "low" by comparison to the 1918 flu, the psychological impact of this disease became its most prescient feature.

The "iron lung" that became widely available in the 1930s stopped asphyxiation of polio victims, and it was a triumph of innovation; it allowed a dramatic reduction in the death rate.[150] Finally, by 1954, a vaccine was developed (by private labs with very little government support subsidies) and the disease was largely eradicated in the US twenty years later. It became a signature achievement of the medical industry and the promise of vaccines.

Here is the data on infection and death:[151]

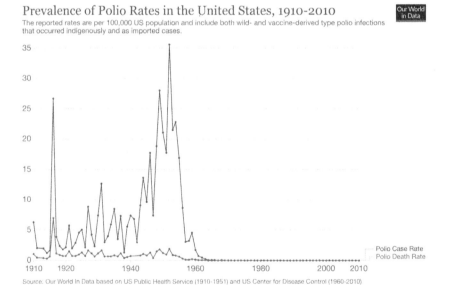

Prevalence of Polio Rates in the United States, 1910-2010

The reported rates are per 100,000 US population and include both wild- and vaccine-derived type polio infections that occurred indigenously and as imported cases.

Source: Our World In Data based on US Public Health Service (1910-1951) and US Center for Disease Control (1960-2010)
OurWorldInData.org/polio/ • CC BY

---

150 Wikipedia. 2020. "Iron lung." *Wikipedia*, May 9.

151 Our World in Data. n.d. "Prevalence of Polio Rates in the United States, 1910-2010." *Our World in Data.*

Throughout the country, the quarantining of the sick was deployed in a limited way as one medical response. There were some shutdowns. The CDC reports that "travel and commerce between affected cities were sometimes restricted [by local officials].[152] Public health officials imposed quarantines (used to separate and restrict the movement of well people who may have been exposed to a contagious disease to see if they become ill) on homes and towns where polio cases were diagnosed."

President Harry Truman spoke frequently about the need for a national mobilization against polio.[153] But what he meant by this was to rally people to be cautious, follow medical guidelines, isolate the infected, and get the medical community inspired to find means of treatment and cure. Though there was no cure, and no vaccine, there was a long incubation period before symptoms would reveal themselves, and while there was a great deal of confusion about how it was transmitted, the thought of locking down an entire state, nation, or world was inconceivable. The concept of a universal "shelter-in-place" order was nowhere imaginable. Efforts to impose "social distancing" were selective and voluntary.

In an earlier 1937 outbreak in Chicago, for example, the superintendent of schools (not the mayor or governor) closed the public schools for three weeks and encouraged learning from home.[154] In many localities, when there was an outbreak and depending on the level of fear, bowling alleys and movie theaters were closed, but not by force.[155] Church services were cancelled sporadically, but not by force. The churches themselves were never shuttered.

In Minnesota in 1948, the state board of health cautioned against going ahead with the state fair. It was cancelled. In 1950, James Magrath,

---

152 CDC. 2019. "Polio Elimination in the United States." *Centers for Disease Control and Prevention*, October 25.

153 Truman Library. 2019. "Poliomyelitis." *Harry S. Truman Library*; 1964. *Public Papers of the Presidents of the United States: Harry S. Truman 1949.* United States Government Printing Office. See p. 471.

154 Strauss, Valerie. 2020. "In Chicago, schools closed during a 1937 polio epidemic and kids learned from home - over the radio." *The Washington Post*, April 3.

155 Oshinsky, David. 2014. "Remembering the dreaded summers of polio." *Elsevier Connect*, October 22.

president of the Minnesota state board of health warned against large gatherings, and regretted how much people persisted in gatherings of children, but added:[156] "Nobody can shut down intercourse of people in communities… We will just have to say, 'Do everything you can within reason.' You can't close up everything…'"

In May 1949, after an outbreak in San Angelo, Texas (my father remembers this), the city council voted (voted!) to close all indoor meeting places for one week, according to the wonderful book *Polio: An American Story* by David M. Oshinsky, with a promised ending period.[157] But the local epidemic didn't pass that quickly, and by June hospitals were filled with patients. Tourism stopped because people didn't want to be there. Cleaning fanaticism was the rule of the day. Most indoor theaters and bowling alleys stayed closed simply because people were afraid (no evidence of any prosecutions). In the end, writes Oshinsky, "San Angelo saw 420 cases, one for every 124 inhabitants, of whom 84 were permanently paralyzed and 28 died." And by August, polio was gone again. Life in San Angelo gradually returned to normal.

This experience repeated itself in most places in the country where there were outbreaks. City councils would encourage the following of the directives of the National Foundation for Infantile Paralysis (later the March of Dimes), which circulated a list of "polio precautions" for parents to follow. Some towns and cities across the United States tried to prevent the spread of polio by closing swimming pools, libraries, and movie theaters (not restaurants or barber shops) on a temporary basis but mostly in a way consistent with the public mood stemming from fear and confusion.

The only protests against authorities in a half-century of confusion came in New York when it seemed in the 1910s that authorities were targeting immigrant children with a burdensome demand that they be polio-free before integrating themselves into the community. "If you report any more of our babies to the Board of Health," wrote the Italian Black Hand

---

156 Emmerson, Elisabeth. 2009. Chapter 3 "Polio: Minnesota's Crucial Role." In *Public Health is People: A History of the Minnesota Department of Health from 1949 to 1999.*

157 Oshinsky, David M. 2005. "Polio: An American Story." *Oxford University Press*: New York, NY.

in blood, "we will kill you."

What's remarkable in light of the near-global coercive lockdown for Covid-19 is how the terrible and terrifying disease of polio was managed almost entirely by a private and voluntary system of health professionals, innovators, parental responsibility, localized caution, and individual volition and caution where needed. It was an imperfect system because the virus was so vicious, cruel, and random. But precisely because there were no national or state lockdowns — and only very limited local closures done mostly in a way consistent with citizen fear — the system remained adaptive to changing conditions.

Meanwhile, "Guys and Dolls" and "The King and I" appeared on Broadway, "A Streetcar Named Desire" and "African Queen" rocked the movie theaters, the steel mills hummed as never before, the oil industry boomed, domestic and international travel continued to roar and become democratized, the civil rights movement was born, and the "golden age of American capitalism" took root, all in the thick of a terrible disease.

This was a time when, even for this ghastly disease that maimed innocent young children, medical problems were widely seen to have medical solutions and not political ones. Yes, there were clear policy responses to these past pandemics, but they targeted the most vulnerable populations to keep them safe, while leaving everyone else alone. Polio was especially bad for school children, but that meant they closed the schools temporarily, in cooperation with parents and the community. The current pandemic is different because, instead of targeting the vulnerable populations, we've gone for society-wide one size fits all at nearly the national and global level, and certainly the state level. That's never happened — not with polio, not with the Spanish flu, the 1957 flu, the 1968 flu, or anything else.

As the health official quote above said of the polio epidemic: "Nobody can shut down intercourse of people in communities." Our rights survived. So did human liberty, free enterprise, the Bill of Rights, jobs, and the American way of life. And then polio was eventually eradicated. The slogan for polio eradication — "Do everything you can within reason" — seems like a good rule of thumb for the management of future pandemics.

Elvis Was King, Ike Was President, and 116,000 Americans Died in a Pandemic

The year was 1957. Elvis's new movie "Jailhouse Rock" was packing the theaters. The last episode of "I Love Lucy" aired on television. The show "West Side Story" held tryouts in Washington, D.C., and opened on Broadway in September. Ford's new car the Edsel rolled off the assembly line. The Cold War with Russia was on and "In God We Trust" appeared on US currency. The first Toys 'R' Us store opened. Also that year, the so-called Asian Flu killed 116,000 Americans. Here is the full summary from the Centers for Disease Control:[158]

> In February 1957, a new influenza A (H2N2) virus emerged in East Asia, triggering a pandemic ("Asian Flu"). This H2N2 virus was comprised of three different genes from an H2N2 virus that originated from an avian influenza A virus, including the H2 hemagglutinin and the N2 neuraminidase genes. It was first reported in Singapore in February 1957, Hong Kong in April 1957, and in coastal cities in the United States in summer 1957. The estimated number of deaths was 1.1 million worldwide and 116,000 in the United States.

Like the current pandemic, there was a demographic pattern to the deaths. It hit the elderly population with heart and lung disease. In a frightening twist, the virus could also be fatal for pregnant women. The

---

158 CDC. n.d. "1957-1958 Pandemic (H2N2 virus)." *Centres for Disease Control and Prevention (CDC)*.

infection rate was probably even higher than the Spanish flu of 1918 (675,000 Americans died from this), but this lowered the overall case fatality rate to 0.67%.[159] A vaccine became available in late 1957 but was not widely distributed. The population of the US at the time was 172 million, which is a little more than half of the current population. Life expectancy was 69 as versus 78 in 2020. Even with shorter lives, it was a healthier population with lower rates of obesity. To extrapolate the data to a counterfactual, we can conclude that this virus was more wicked than Covid-19 thus far.

What's remarkable when we look back to 1957, nothing was shut down. Restaurants, schools, theaters, sporting events, travel — everything continued without interruption. Without a 24-hour news cycle with thousands of news agencies and a billion websites hungry for traffic, mostly people paid no attention other than to keep basic hygiene. It was covered in the press as a medical problem. The notion that there was a political solution never occurred to anyone.[160] Again, this was a very serious flu, and it persisted for 10 years until it mutated to become the Hong Kong flu of 1968.[161]

The *New York Times* had some, but not much, coverage. On September 18, 1957, an editorial counseled: "Let us all keep a cool head about Asian influenza as the statistics on the spread and the virulence of the disease begin to accumulate. For one thing, let us be sure that the 1957 type of A influenza virus is innocuous, as early returns show, and that antibiotics can indeed control the complications that may develop."

The mystery of why today vast numbers of governments around the world (but not all) have crushed economies, locked people under house

---

159 Wikipedia. 2020. "1957–1958 influenza pandemic." *Wikipedia*, May 7.

160 **Note of correction:** A correspondent pointed out to me that "The October 1957 LDS General Conference was cancelled because of the flu epidemic in 1957 and there may have been other organizations that did so." I'm grateful for the correction, and it makes the point: society was not ignorant of the pandemic. Instead, there were a variety of intelligent responses depending on the risk. I'm speculating that this event would have included quite a number of people on the list of the vulnerable.

161 See article herein entitled, "Woodstock Occurred in the Middle of a Pandemic."

arrest, wrecked business, spread despair, disregarded basic freedoms and rights will require years — if not decades — to sort out. Is it the news cycle that is creating mass hysteria? Political ambition and arrogance? A decline in philosophical regard for freedom as the best system for dealing with crises? Most likely, the ultimate answer will look roughly like what historians say about the Great War (WWI): it was a perfect storm that created a calamity that no one intended at the outset.

For staying calm and treating the terrible Asian flu of 1957 as a medical problem to address with medical intelligence, rather than as an excuse to unleash Medieval-style brutality, this first postwar generation deserves our respect and admiration.

Woodstock Occurred in the Middle of a Pandemic

I n my lifetime, there was another deadly flu epidemic in the United States. The flu spread from Hong Kong to the United States, arriving in December 1968, and peaked a year later. It ultimately killed 100,000 people in the US, mostly over the age of 65, and one million worldwide.

Lifespan in the US in those days was 70 whereas it is 78 in 2020. Population was 200 million as compared with 328 million in 2020. It was also a healthier population with low obesity.[162] If it were possible to extrapolate the death data based on population and demographics, we might be looking at a quarter million deaths today from this virus. So in terms of lethality, it was as deadly and scary as Covid-19 if not more so, though we shall have to wait to see.

"In 1968," says Nathaniel L. Moir in *National Interest*, "the H3N2 pandemic killed more individuals in the US than the combined total number of American fatalities during both the Vietnam and Korean Wars."[163] And this happened in the lifetimes of every American over 52 years of age. I was 5 years old and have no memory of this at all. My mother vaguely remembers being careful and washing surfaces, and encouraging her mom and dad to be careful. Otherwise, it's mostly forgotten today. Why is that?

---

162 Wikipedia. 2016. "Graph: Obesity rates of adult males, 1960–2015." *Wikipedia*.

163 Moir, Nathaniel L. 2020. "Move Over, Coronavirus: We Fought A Pandemic During the Vietnam War." *The National Interest*, April 24.

Nothing was closed by force. Schools mostly stayed open.[164] Businesses too. You could go to the movies. You could go to bars and restaurants. John Fund has a friend who reports having attended a Grateful Dead concert.[165] In fact, people have no memory or awareness that the famous Woodstock concert of August 1969 — planned in January during the worst period of death — actually occurred during a deadly American flu pandemic that only peaked globally six months later. There was no thought given to the virus which, like ours today, was dangerous mainly for a non-concert-going demographic.

Stock markets didn't crash. Congress passed no legislation. The Federal Reserve did nothing. Not a single governor acted to enforce social distancing, curve flattening (even though hundreds of thousands of people were hospitalized), or banning of crowds. No mothers were arrested for taking their kids to other homes. No surfers were arrested. No daycares were shut even though there were more infant deaths with this virus than the one we are experiencing now. There were no suicides, no unemployment, no drug overdoses. Media covered the pandemic but it never became a big issue.

As Bojan Pancevski in the *Wall Street Journal* points out, "In 1968-70, news outlets devoted cursory attention to the virus while training their lenses on other events such as the moon landing and the Vietnam War, and the cultural upheaval of the civil-rights movements, student protests and the sexual revolution."[166]

The only actions governments took were to collect data, watch and wait, encourage testing and vaccines, and so on. The medical community took

---

164 Note: an earlier version said no schools closed. But a reader pointed me to an academic article that says "23 [states] faced school and college closures" but implies that this was due to absenteeism. This further underscores how aware people were at the time of the disease; the stay-open practice was a deliberate choice. See: Jester, Barbara J., Timothy M. Uyeki & Daniel B. Jernigan. 2020. "Fifty Years of Influenza A(H3N2) Following the Pandemic of 1968." *American Journal of Public Health*, 110(5): 669-676.

165 Fund, John. 2020. "The Forgotten Hong Kong Flu Pandemic of 1968 Has Lessons for Today." *National Review*, April 26.

166 Pancevski, Bojan. 2020. "Forgotten Pandemic Offers Contrast to Today's Coronavirus Lockdowns." *The Wall Street Journal*, April 24.

the primary responsibility for disease mitigation, as one might expect. It was widely assumed that diseases require medical, not political, responses. It's not as if we had governments unwilling to intervene in other matters. We had the Vietnam War, social welfare, public housing, urban renewal, and the rise of Medicare and Medicaid. We had a president swearing to cure all poverty, illiteracy, and disease. Government was as intrusive as it had ever been in history. But for some reason, there was no thought given to shutdowns. Which raises the question: why was Covid-19 different? We will be trying to figure this one out for decades.

Was the difference that we have mass media invading our lives with endless notifications blowing up in our pockets? Was there some change in philosophy such that we now think politics is responsible for all existing aspects of life? Was there a political element here in that the media blew this wildly out of proportion as revenge against Trump and his deplorables? Or did our excessive adoration of predictive modelling get out of control to the point that we let a physicist with ridiculous models frighten the world's governments into violating the human rights of billions of people?[167] Maybe all of these were factors. Or maybe there is something darker and nefarious at work, as the conspiracy theorists would have it. Regardless, they all have some explaining to do.

By way of personal recollection, my own mother and father were part of a generation that believed they had developed sophisticated views of viruses. They understood that less vulnerable people getting them not only strengthened immune systems but contributed to disease mitigation by reaching "herd immunity." They had a whole protocol to make a child feel better about being sick. I got a "sick toy," unlimited ice cream, Vicks rub on my chest, a humidifier in my room, and so on. They would constantly congratulate me on building immunity. They did their very best to be happy about my viruses, while doing their best to get me through them.

If we used government lockdowns then like we use them now, Woodstock (which changed music forever and still resonates today) would never have occurred. How much prosperity, culture, tech, etc. are

---

167 Magness, Phillip W. 2020. "How Wrong Were the Models and Why?" *American Institute for Economic Research*, April 23.

we losing in this calamity? What happened between then and now? Was there some kind of lost knowledge, as happened with scurvy, when we once had sophistication and then the knowledge was lost and had to be re-found?[168] For Covid-19, we reverted to medieval-style understandings and policies, even in the 21st century. It's all very strange. The contrast between 1968 and 2020 couldn't be more striking. They were smart. We are idiots. Or at least our governments are.

---

168 Higgins, Chris. 2010. "How Scurvy Was Cured, then the Cure Was Lost." *MentalFloss,* March 8.

That Time Jesus Was Quarantined

Most of us didn't realize, until very recently, what a remarkable stain is put upon a person (or whole people) said to be diseased. Even people who have had the coronavirus and recovered (as 99% do) are right now regarded as suspect and treated as we imagine lepers were in the old days.

The biases have been unreal, and the policies based on those actions extreme. It began with banning flights from China, and then Europe, UK, and Australia, forcing chaos and social closening in airports all over the country. Then the separationism came home. State borders closed. Then it got even closer to home. Next town? Stay out. Next block? Stay away. Next door in my apartment complex? Stay away from my front door. Not even spouses and children are safe. Everyone stay away from everyone else and douse yourself constantly with a cleansing agent.

Observers are warning that all borders, not just national ones, are hardening, just as they did during and following World War II – at great cost to liberty and prosperity. When you look at the incredible fear, paranoia, and loathing that the coronavirus has unleashed, you get a glimpse of what must have been a long-time human habit of suspecting others of passing on diseases. There is a remarkable power in that, especially if it only amounts to suspicion, rumor, bias, and smear, and it would naturally affect people who are different in other ways: foreign, different language, different social class, a different income group.

J. Duncan M. Derrett wrote in 1987, the disease called leprosy in the

Bible was associated with the revelation of hidden sin.[169] Anyone suspected of carrying it was banned from the temple, not just for reasons of disease control but even more for maintaining the moral purity of the space. It was common for anyone deemed a sinner to be tagged with the label leper rightly or wrongly. He or she would be forced to seek some kind of healing in order to be able to gain access again and not forever be socially distanced. Until then, anyone who came near him was also considered unclean. They were forced into isolation, which could mean emotional and physical death.

Then as now, the appearance of pandemic is a perfect mechanism for turning people against each other, and for power to grow, with shocking results. It will forever be etched in the annals of history that in 2020 Christians themselves were banned from their churches all over the world – on Easter Sunday – for fear of disease. Thinking about this brings to mind this passage from St. Mark, Chapter 1, verses 40-45.[170]

And there came a leper to him, beseeching him, and kneeling down to him, and saying unto him, If thou wilt, thou canst make me clean.

41 And Jesus, moved with compassion, put forth his hand, and touched him, and saith unto him, I will; be thou clean.

42 And as soon as he had spoken, immediately the leprosy departed from him, and he was cleansed.

43 And he straitly charged him, and forthwith sent him away;

44 And saith unto him, See thou say nothing to any man: but go thy way, shew thyself to the priest, and offer for thy cleansing those things which Moses commanded, for a testimony unto them.

169 Derrett, J. Duncan M. 1987. "No Stone Upon Another: Leprosy and the Temple." *Journal for the Study of the New Testament*, 9(3): 3-20.

170 Derrett, J. Duncan M. 1987. "No Stone Upon Another: Leprosy and the Temple." *Journal for the Study of the New Testament*, 9(30): 3-20.

45 But he went out, and began to publish it much, and to blaze abroad the matter, insomuch that Jesus could no more openly enter into the city, but was without in desert places: and they came to him from every quarter.

There is another problem with the designation leper. Scholars who study this stuff find no evidence of anything we call leprosy at that time at that place. Since the 1950s, medical historians have been explaining this, as summed up by E.V Hulse in 1975:[171]

> From the medical, historical, and paleopathological evidence it is clear that biblical "leprosy" is not modern leprosy. There are no indications whatsoever that the disease we now know as leprosy was not present in the Near East in Old Testament times and descriptions of 'sara' are not accepted by experienced leprologists as having any relationship to modern leprosy.

Same with the New Testament: "Not only are there no clinical descriptions of 'lepra' in the New Testament," he writes, "but the use of the word lepra is, in itself, strong evidence that the New Testament 'leprosy' was not modern leprosy." It might have been a scaly skin rash, or it might have been something one just says about another who is different. Once there is a rumor of disease, everyone is a suspect. If suspicion fell upon any person, it was difficult to escape. People talk. People fear. They want that person out of sight and out of mind. Then as now. Especially without testing!

All of which is to say that the man Jesus confronted might not have had any real disease at all, but he was still banned from the temple as generally unclean. So when Jesus the Rabbi pronounced him clean, he might have been pronouncing him so as an act of compassion and love. But Jesus was also a practical man. He suggested that the now-clean man go through ritual cleansing. He also pleaded with the man: please don't tell anyone that Jesus touched him. The guy did it anyway. Whoops!

---

171 "King James Version: Mark 1:40-45." *Bible Gateway*.

Next thing you know, "Jesus could no more openly enter into the city, but was without in desert places." Yes, you know how this works. You got near a corona person who is probably that because he was near a corona person, and then that person got near you and now you are suddenly suspected. To the 14-day quarantine for you buddy! The good news is that despite the quarantine Jesus' ministry endured, "They came to him from every quarter."

This is fully consistent with everything we know about Jesus's ministry. The parables and his life narrative are full of stories of breaking down biases, barriers, myths, and artificial walls of tribes, religion, class, gender, and political loyalty. He told of the good Samaritan who helped a stranger. He washed the feet of the poor. He defended a prostitute against stoning. He told his followers to pray for the imprisoned and saved the soul even of a tax collector. So too did he use his influence to remove the stigma of presence or rumor of disease.

Our times have reminded us that being called diseased is like other forms of social division that drive people apart and make them more dependent on power. It leads people to fear, hate, and separate. Jesus too not only addressed that topic; he lived it, even at the penalty of personal quarantine. He healed the lepers simply by declaring them clean, which is to say that he gave them a pass to re-enter society.[172] It was a similar situation with Simon the Leper with whom Jesus ate (Mark 14:3-9).[173] As it turns out, Simon didn't actually have leprosy (well, no one did but he might once have been sick thus earning him the lifetime moniker, poor guy), so even getting well doesn't give a once-sick person a free pass. Jesus, however, didn't care: his job was to ennoble not vilify.

We are learning so much in our times. We thought we had seen every conceivable excuse for liberty to decline and power to rise. Financial crisis, terrorism, inequality, injustice, discrimination, microaggression, cultural appropriation, globalism; you name it, we've lived it. Every time there is a crisis, we are told the same thing: you can't be free; instead you

---

172 "King James Version: Luke 17." Bible Gateway.

173 Wikia. 2020. "Simon the Leper." *Religion Wiki.*

must obey. What we've not seen and lived through until now is the ancient tendency to wreck social cooperation through the rumor and reality of disease. Jesus, however, did see that. He dealt with it with compassion, moral courage, and patience. May we all live and learn.

Our Ten Days that Shook the World

Jack Reed, the American communist who was buried in the Kremlin, is the author of the extremely exciting book *Ten Days that Shook the World*.[174] It's about the Bolshevik Revolution which is witnessed first hand, and he was a huge fan who turned out to be one of many of its victims. But his book is also about any time of astonishing upheaval, times like our own when history seems to turn on a dime in ways no one expected. A quasi-free society became a fully planned one, under the control of an elite who claimed the mantle of science.

We are living through something similar. The results have been similarly disappointing. We tried to "flatten the curve" to preserve hospital capacity, but this is just a fancy way of saying "prolong the pain." It was a form of rationing access to medical services, seemingly necessary given the scoliosis of this highly regulated industrial sector. But the political class and their modelers only considered one kind of pain. Other forms of pain are already here in the form of mass unemployment, waves of bankruptcy, rising despair, social division and anger, a panicked political class, and a seething fury on the part of millions of people — who had long taken their right to work and associate as a given — who suddenly find themselves under house arrest.

Going through my personal financial statements for the last 30 days, I'm reminded of how this nightmare unfolded. My last trip to the old (pre-lockdown) New York was on March 12, 2020. I was with AIER's videographer Taleed Brown. The virus was all the talk but the city hadn't shut down yet. There were fewer cars on the road, fewer people by half walking around. The bars were full, stuffed with people even at 11:00am

174 Reed, John. 1919. *Ten Days that Shook the World*. International Publishers: New York, NY.

who had some sense that this might be their last drink. Groups of 4 and 6 were sitting around talking and trying to celebrate birthdays and pretend things were normal, as best they could.

But things weren't normal. I was there for a 4pm television interview, and I had 5 hours to wait for it. I worried that the Amtrak would stop running before we could catch it home. We would be trapped. So the minutes went by for hours. Taleed and I sat there eating and drinking but even at the Irish Pub, things were different. There were paper tablecloths where there used to be exposed wood. Our server stood far away and set our drinks and food down on the table next to us. She had a look of impending doom of her face, as she confronted two possible disasters: getting sick and getting shut down.

How far along had the disease progressed at that point? The first US case of Covid-19 was reported on January 20, 2020, in Washington State.[175] No one knows how many other cases there were already spreading through the Northeast of the US. Thousands? Millions? Many cases have no symptoms. Others feel like a minor cold. Others are taken down for a couple of days. Do you tell others and get tested every time you feel sick? No. The virus might already have been everywhere in New York when I was there.

The interview finally came and went and we rushed to the train station to get home as soon as possible. Were we carrying infection? I had no idea. There were no means to find out. Even after all this time, there still is no widespread testing outside of hospitals. If CVS did offer the test, there would be a line down the block. The fateful disaster of the CDC/FDA to botch the creation and distribution of tests is still present in our lives.[176] We still don't know. Amazing.

After that day in New York, our worlds began to shut down. The following day, a national emergency was declared. Then the CDC recommended against gatherings of 50 or more people. France locked down.

---

175 Holshue, Michelle L., Chas DeBolt, Scott Lindquist et al. 2020. "First Case of 2019 Novel Coronavirus in the United States." *The New England Journal of Medicine*, March 5, 382: 929-936.

176 Thierer, Adam. 2020. "How the US Botched Coronavirus Testing." *American Institute for Economic Research*, March 12.

Borders closed. Then the unthinkable scenario unfolded: stores shut, borders shut, police-enforced stay-at-home orders, mass unemployment, family bankruptcy, psychological depression, a nation of prisoners in our homes. Spooky doesn't describe it. Not one person in the US imagined this was possible, and I'm speaking as a person who warned of coming quarantines on January 27, 2020. Back then, I wrote the following:[177]

> Remember that it is not government that discovers the disease, treats the disease, keeps diseased patients from wandering around, or otherwise compels sick people to decline to escape their sick beds. Institutions do this, institutions that are part of the social order and not exogenous to it.
>
> Individuals don't like to get others sick. People don't like to get sick. Given this, we have a mechanism that actually works. Society has an ability and power of its own to bring about quarantine-like results without introducing the risk that the State's quarantine power will be used and abused for political purposes.

But the political class in the United States (unlike Sweden and South Korea) didn't trust society.[178] Oh, to be sure, society was trusted to adapt to the most astonishing series of mandates, burdens, and shifts in modern history. The whole of the industrial structure was massively contorted, distorted, and violently attacked. And yet the grocery stores and pharmacies, plus all their suppliers, proved unbelievably adaptable, people became specialists in distancing, and millions learned about remote work and digital hangouts.

The political elites and their plans for us just assumed society was capable of this, and they were right. But if society could achieve this level of upheaval in the course of a week, how much more capable would it

---

177 Tucker, Jeffrey A. 2020. "Must Government Save Us from the Coronavirus?" *American Institute for Economic Research*, January 27.

178 Book, Joakim. 2020. "What Sweden Has Done Right on Coronavirus." *American Institute for Economic Research*, March 31; Earle, Peter C. 2020. "South Korea Preserved the Open Society and Now Infection Rates are Falling." *American Institute for Economic Research*, March 12.

have been in dealing with a disease itself — and dare I suggest deal with the disease better than the politicians ever could. This is precisely why 800 serious medical professionals begged and pleaded to stop the lockdown before it happened.[179]

The trouble I had from the beginning with this whole central plan to flatten the curve — we cannot know if it is happening much less why, simply because we have neither data nor a clear test of cause and effect — is that central plans have never worked. They are hugely costly in ways that models cannot predict.[180] Meanwhile, the medical professionals discovered features of this disease that are distinct and should have informed policy decisions.[181] Even after the shutdown, some politicians began to doubt.[182] "If you rethought that or had time to analyze that public health strategy," said New York Governor Andrew Cuomo, "I don't know that you would say 'quarantine everyone.' I don't even know that that was the best public health policy." By then it was too late.

But let's return to Jack Reed and his dreams for a communist world, starting with Russia. I recently re-watched the film *Reds*.[183] After all these years, the movie holds up as one of the most intellectually interesting and visually powerful portrayals of lost history that I've seen. The movie stars Warren Beatty playing John Reed, while Diane Keaton plays his girlfriend and eventual wife, Louise Bryant. It includes some of the best romantic fight scenes I've ever seen, not least because they paralleled the actual off-screen lives of Beatty and Keaton. The portrayals of figures like Max

---

179 Stringham, Edward Peter. 2020. "800 Medical Specialists Caution Against Draconian Measures." *American Institute for Economic Research*, March 24.

180 Luther, William J. 2020. "More Sensational Reporting on COVID-19 Estimates." *American Institute for Economic Research*, March 27.

181 Tucker, Jeffrey A. 2020. "With Knowledge Comes Calm, Rationality, and, Possibly, Openness." *American Institute for Economic Research*, April 5.

182 Tucker, Jeffrey A. 2020. "We Were Wrong: So Sorry that We Ruined Your Life." *American Institute for Economic Research*, March 28.

183 Beatty, Warren. 1981. *Reds*. Film. Directed by Warren Beatty. US: Paramount Pictures.

Eastman, Eugene O'Neill, and Emma Goldman are very convincing.[184]

In terms of culture and politics, the film provides a richer education than you can get from 50 books on the topic of the Progressive Era, the Great War, the Russian Revolution, and the heady brew of interwoven cultural issues like women's suffrage, birth control, abortion, free love, and the beginnings of the organized socialist movement in the United States.

I've never been sympathetic to the Bolsheviks as versus the old regime in Russia, but the scenes here from the revolution are completely inspired and touch the heart of anyone who agrees with Jefferson on the positive need for revolution from time to time. The portrayals of both Lenin and Trotsky seem authentic, and thrillingly so.

That sense you get that you are watching the real thing is enhanced by the extended interviews with people who actually knew both Reed and Bryant. They all have strong opinions. They are wise. They are insightful. We hear from communists and anticommunists, socialites and politicians, working-class philosophers and credentialed academics. It is a beautiful mix.

From a political perspective, the film offers a devastating turnaround judgment on the results of revolution. Emma Goldman tries to talk some sense into Reed in the years following, and explains that millions have died from starvation, that nothing works right, that the vanguard of the proletariat has become a centralized police state. Reed won't listen. He explains back to her that the socialist revolution requires terror, murder, and firing squads. Here is the exchange with Maureen Stapleton playing Emma Goldman:

> **Goldman:** "Jack, we have to face it. The dream that we had is dying. If Bolshevism means the peasants taking the land, the workers taking the factories, then Russia's one place where there is no Bolshevism."

> **Reed:** "Ya know, I can argue with cops. I can fight with generals. I can't deal with a bureaucrat."

---

184 FEE. n.d. "Max Forrester Eastman." *Foundation for Economic Education.*

Goldman: "You think Zinoviev is nothing worse than a bureaucrat. The Soviets have no local autonomy. The central state has all the power. All the power is in the hands of a few men and they are destroying the revolution. They are destroying any hope of real communism in Russia. They are putting people like me in jail. My understanding of revolution is not a continual extermination of political dissenters. And I want no part of it. Every single newspaper has been shut down or taken over by the Party. Anyone even vaguely suspected of being a counter-revolutionary can be taken out and shot without a trial. Where does it end? Is any nightmare justifiable in the name of defense against counter-revolution? The dream may be dying in Russia, but I'm not. It may take some time, but I'm getting out."

Reed: "You sound like you are a little confused about the revolution in action, EG. Up 'till now you've only dealt with it in theory. What did you think this thing was going to be? A revolution by consensus where we all sat down and agreed over a cup of coffee?"

Goldman: "Nothing works! Four million people died last year. Not from fighting war, they died from starvation and typhus in a militaristic police state that suppresses freedom and human rights — where nothing works!"

Reed: "They died because of the French, British and American blockade that cut off all food and medical supplies. And, counter-revolutionaries have sabotaged the factories and the railroads and telephones. And the people, the poor, ignorant, superstitious, illiterate people are trying to run things themselves just like you always said they should, but they don't know how to run them yet. Did you honestly think things were going to work right away? Did you honestly expect social transformation was going to be anything other than a murderous process? It's a war

EG, and we got to fight it like we fight a war: with discipline, with terror, with firing squads. Or we just give it up."

Goldman: "Those four million didn't die fighting a war. They died from a system that cannot work."

Reed: "It's just the beginning, EG. It's not happening like we thought it would. It's not happening the way we wanted it to, but it is happening. If you walk out on it now, what does your whole life mean?"

And here we come to understand something of the strange mind of the dedicated communist ideologue, so dogmatic in his adherence to a creed that nothing can shake his faith, not even the deaths of millions and millions of people. His doubts about the revolution and the Communist Party crystallize only when one of his speeches is edited. So he can turn a blind eye to holocaust, but a violation of his freedom to speak becomes an intolerable act. Some moral compass!

The entire story makes an interesting parallel with our own times. The barren predictive models on how many would die from Covid-19 felt like science but their range of predictions made them useless in practice. It would be like a weather prediction that said: either your house will completely flood or there will be a light drizzle, depending on whether you do the following Kabuki dance. Still, the media howled and the politicians acted in extreme ways to protect their standing with voters (or so they believed then).

What they hadn't considered were a number of possibilities: the models weren't predictive, curve flattening is pain prolonging, Covid-19 doesn't spontaneously appear just because people are in groups, nothing about staying home is going to cause the virus to get bored and go away, the costs of unemployment and bankruptcy are astonishingly high, school closings put older vulnerable people in direct contact with children who do not suffer the effects of infection, and the whole reaction was based on a presumption that human rights and the Constitution do not matter. It was brutal, irrational, medieval, and eschewed the advice of the best and most learned minds in epidemiology. They created madness and destruction and called it health.

At the end of this, there will still be Goldmans and Reeds, people who admit errors and those who will stick by their guns, humble minds who will see that there were better ways and arrogant fools who will keep screaming that setting the world on fire was all we could do.

The Goldmans will say: millions suffered not from the virus but from the response to the virus. Meanwhile, we threw out every principle of human decency, freedom, property, and science.

The Reeds will say: It didn't happen like we thought it would, but it happened. If you reject it now, what does your whole life mean?

The Hope

America Rediscovers Empathy

From early in the lockdown days, it became clear that this crisis would not make us "come together" and be "better people." It would not be like 9-11. Instead, it would shatter our lives and make us worse people. We would turn on each other, engage in dramatic deeds that would hurt and harm people we like and love, and push our political agendas ahead of basic humane values. Dogs eating dogs, suitable for a people muscled and bludgeoned as if we are animals.

Massive state intervention unleashes all kinds of hell, and this is one kind. An example here has been the shocking lack of empathy that people have shown toward the plight of others over these months. I had people tell me the "lockdowns have been just fine" for them – because they are stay home people, have a cool tech job or whatever – and therefore all the anger about the lockdowns is completely overwrought. They tried to pass this off as doing good for others, and even the government awarded them points for staying home.

What about a bit of empathy for the waiters, actors, musicians, athletes, hotel workers, airline employees, and all the technicians associated with all affected industries, who saw massive financial losses and job losses? Not a tear shed for the small business owner wrecked. No concern for the parents who have their children's schools closed. And who could possibly care about the millions locked out of their churches on Easter?

Apparently, there is a whole class of people out there who are just thrilled to work in their PJs and expect the world to deliver unto them food, liquor, electricity, music, and high-speed internet, just so long as everyone else is out there hustling to make it all happen. They looked at the protests against the lockdown and said: "Hey, they should stay home and be a hero like me! What's wrong with these people?" Certainly most mainstream reporters seemed to hold this view. The protesters back then were bad guys while the compliant stay-at-homers were the good guys. I would suggest the opposite is closer to truth: the protesters were those who showed empathy for others, and also moral courage in the face of media attacks.

To sit at home in those days, like some 18th century French court aristocrat, and sneer at those who were out doing good – exercising their freedoms and rights to help others regain theirs – suggests a dark worldview, almost pathological; it shows a fundamentally anti-social outlook of selfishness and disregard for the millions (and billions) who have suffered so much from the coercive shutdowns. You see the same lack of concern for others in the models that drove the closures in the first place. They treated human beings as nothing but data to manipulate and then sloganize to make us comply.

A pretty important basis of civilization is the capacity of a people to tie their personal happiness to the awareness of the possibility of happiness of others too. Systematic injustice and oppression should trouble us, and inspire us to do something about it. The mandatory closures and vicious division between essential and nonessential people amounted to that. This is why the George Floyd protests — not the riots but the protests — were so hugely important to breaking out of this immoral indifference to the plight of others. It was the moment when Americans finally rediscovered their capacity for empathy, after six months in which it was beaten out of them. We looked at the cop's knee on the man's neck and, though the racial element here is very obvious, the oppression at the hands of rulers is a universal experience. It could have been any one of us.

Sometimes experiencing injustice ourselves is the most direct path to gaining an understanding of what others go through. It was my first experience of being arrested (for nothing) and being thrown behind bars that put my own passion for emancipation of everyone into high gear. After that, I wrote about the topic of liberty with new fire. It was the single most influential thing to occur in my adult years.

So too for millions of people, the lockdowns have given them new awareness of the disproportionate power of politicians and the police state. It will not be forgotten. It will likely change this country for decades. To be sure, for many people, these protests are just the fashionable thing to do, just another way to virtue signal. To this I would say: it is in fact a virtue to care about someone besides yourself, to feel pain in the presence of suffering even if it is not against you, to give of your time and energy to making the world a less violent place, in everyone's interest.

For all the people who felt so "virtuous" about staying home and sneering at those who hated the lockdown, I would say that is not virtuous. It is scary and dangerous. Finally being out on the streets, caring about others while exercising our rights; that is indeed making us better people. We are also better people if we celebrate the business owners who make it through this hell, congratulate everyone who did not or could not "stay home," while casting aspersions on any politician who continues to keep restrictions in place.

Having empathy, suggests Adam Smith, is a foundational principle of life and the basis of being a good person.

> How selfish soever man may be supposed, there are evidently some principles in his nature, which interest him in the fortune of others, and render their happiness necessary to him, though he derives nothing from it except the pleasure of seeing it…. As we have no immediate experience of what other men feel, we can form no idea of the manner in which they are affected, but by conceiving what we ourselves should feel in the like situation.

With the reopening and with the street protests around the country, we are rediscovering what it means to have empathy for others and to express that with boldness. Would that we had done so six months ago too. Perhaps we somehow had to go through this time to experience the kind of world in which we do not want to live – closed, cold, cruel – and to remember what we do want for ourselves and country: to be good people who care for others and show it in the warm sunlight of freedom.

Pandemics and the Liberal Path

The record shows that the global economy collapsed not because of the Covid-19 pandemic but because governments around the world, through an astonishing and grossly irresponsible use of coercive power, crushed businesses and supply chains.

Billions of people were suddenly forced into house arrest, government decided what was essential and nonessential, and gatherings of people were regulated to an extreme extent. Thus do we live with the catastrophic results. It's not a great depression. It's a great suppression.[185] Government set out one day suddenly to demolish the very foundations of liberal modernity. And they achieved this with certainty.

But did they save lives? Statisticians can find no difference in excess mortality between countries that locked down and those that did not – just as there is no relationship between a dance I do and whether it rains. Governments around the world embarked on a grand experiment in social control based on unproven theories and using untested methods. It appears as if no good was achieved by any government in terms of disease mitigation. We are left with wrecked prosperity and ruined lives — plus a massive loss in confidence in public sector solutions all over the world.

It's the worst policy of the modern age. And now we are hearing from pundits that the pandemic somehow shows the failure of liberalism. I find this to be a singularly bizarre conclusion. It is not markets which failed but governments. Markets, to the extent they were allowed to exist, gave us food, shelter, and medical care during the worst times. Stock markets

---

185 Epstein, Gene. 2020. "Anatomy of the Great Suppression." *American Institute for Economic Research*, April 9.

continued to function and give us crucial information about resources and valuations. This is a triumph, not a failure.

Perhaps the claim that liberalism has failed is based on the belief that a free society cannot deal with pandemics. In fact, in the course of the 20th century, we have multiple incidences in which disease was handled very well in the context of freedom. Medical professionals got to work and sheltered the vulnerable while mitigating disease through scientific methods. The state stayed out completely in 1949-52, 1957-58, 1968-69, 2006, and 2009. Why we took a different path in 2020 is a mystery. Regardless it was an enormous error.

The great physician Donald Henderson (1928-2016) was responsible for the eradication of smallpox around the world. He was the greatest living expert on pandemics. His view toward quarantines, travel restrictions, school closures, and restrictions on freedom was 100% negative.[186] His principle was that nothing should ever be done to disrupt normal community functioning. Anything government does to restrict people's freedom via coercion risks turning a managed pandemic into a "catastrophe."

That is precisely what has happened. The world will pay the price for decades. This is not the fault of liberalism. It is the fault of terrible decision-making at all levels of society all over the world, with the possible exception of South Korea, Sweden, Japan, and a handful of other countries. This is not a time for more government control. It is time to look again at the foundations of modernity and human rights and once again believe in them and practice them.

As for disease, no one wants to be sick. No one wants to make others sick unnecessarily. If we understand those two truths, we have the basis for understanding how a free society can deal intelligently with the presence of disease. People adapt and learn. Professionals get to work with therapies and finding cures. What precisely governments can contribute to this process is unclear.

---

186 Inglesby, Thomas V., Jennifer B. Nuzzo, Tara O'Toole, and Donald A. Henderson. 2006. "Disease Mitigation Measures in the Control of Pandemic Influenza." *Biosecurity and Bioterrorism: Biodefense Strategy, Practice, and Science*, 4(4): 366-375.

Economist F.A. Hayek spent a lifetime showing that the essential knowledge necessary to cause society to function and thrive resides in the minds of individual actors. Government is not smarter than society. Nothing is gained by pretending otherwise.

What is needed now more than ever is an immediate restoration of free trade, free enterprise, freedom of movement, commercial rights, and human rights. It's a hard truth for governments to admit right now but they have failed all over the world. They need to admit it and leave us alone to restore prosperity and health.[187]

---

187 Carden, Art. 2020. "We Don't Need One Big Plan to End the Lockdown." *American Institute for Economic Research*, May 15.

There Will Be Blowback, In Mostly Good Ways

Back in February, it had been mandatory in my local grocery to use only shopping bags brought from home. Plastic bags were illegal by local ordinance. Then the virus hit. Suddenly the opposite was true. It was illegal to bring bags from home because they could spread disease. Plastic bags were mandatory. As a huge fan of plastic bags, I experienced profound Schadenfreude. It's amazing how the prospect of death clarifies priorities.

Before the virus, we indulged in all sorts of luxuries such as dabbling in dirtiness and imagining a world purified by bucolic naturalness. But when the virus hit, we suddenly realized that a healthy life really matters and that natural things can be very wicked. And then, when government put everyone under house arrest and criminalized freedom itself, we realized many other things too. And we realized them quickly.

Lots of people are predicting how life will fundamentally change in light of our collective experience this last month. I agree but I don't think it will turn out quite as people think. This whole period has been an unconscionable trauma for billions of people, wrecking lives far beyond what even the worst virus could achieve. I'm detecting enormous, unfathomable levels of public fury barely beneath the surface. It won't stay beneath the surface for long.

Our lives in the coming years will be defined by forms of blowback in the wake of both the disease and the egregious policy response, as a much needed corrective. The thing is that you can't take away everyone's rights, put a whole people under house arrest, and abolish the rule of law without generating a response to that in the future.

1. Blowback Against Media

I'm a long-time fan of the *New York Times*. Jeer if you want but I've long admired their reporting, their professionalism, their steady hand, their first draft of history, even if I don't share the paper's center-left political bent.

Something about this virus caused the paper to go completely off the rails. In early March, they began to report on it as if it were the Black Death, suggesting not just closing schools and businesses but actually calling for a complete totalitarian policy.[188] It was shocking and utterly preposterous. The guy who wrote that article has a degree in rhetoric from Berkeley and yet he was calling the shots on the paper's entire response to disease on a national level. They've gone so far as to falsify dates in their reporting in order to manipulate the timeline (I called them out on a case in point; the paper made the change but never admitted the error.[189])

I'm sure that in the coming days and weeks, the paper will dial back all this blather just as they did their certainty that Hillary Clinton would win the 2016 election. In fact, they have already started with an admission that the virus was already widespread in the months before the lockdown (which suggests that almost everything else the paper has written since March has been wrong).[190] But it will be too late. They bear some moral culpability for what has happened to our country.

Anyway, I don't want to pick on the *Times* alone; the media has been nearly in lockstep on the need for lockdown forever and on the claim that this virus is universally lethal for everyone. You can read in various spots

188 McNeil, Donald G., Jr. 2020. "To Take On the Coronavirus, Go Medieval on It." *The New York Times*, February 28.

189 Tucker, Jeffrey A. 2020. "This is a very good piece by @amy_harmon but she gets the date wrong on Fauci's NEJM editorial…" *Twitter*, tweeted April 17.

190 Carey, Benedict, & James Glanz. 2020. "Hidden Outbreaks Spread Through U.S. Cities Far Earlier Than Americans Knew, Estimates Say." *The New York Times*, April 23.

alternative opinions from experts.[191]

Once you get up to speed on the real story here, with authoritative voices, you turn on *Fox*, *CNN*, *NYT*, *CNBC*, and all of the rest (the *WSJ* has been slightly better), and you hear nothing about any of this. They merely spin tales.[192] People glued to the tube have almost no clue about any basics, such as how long the virus has been here, how gigantic is the denominator that makes up the fatality ratio, how many people have zero symptoms so that it's not even an annoyance, the true demographic makeup of the victim population, and the unlikelihood that many of these deaths would have been preventable through any policy.

Watching this disgusting parade of media-driven ignorance, genuine experts or even people passingly curious about data, have become demoralized. Surely many people have already stopped listening to the news completely because it is nothing but a distraction from the reality on the ground.

Why and how did this happen? An obvious answer seems almost too simple: the media wants people at home staring at the television. Maybe that's the whole thing. But it almost seems too cynical to be the full explanation. In any case, I'm not the only one noticing this. I seriously doubt that the credibility of the mainstream media will survive this. There will be blowback. Much needed!

2. Blowback Against Politicians
You do recall, don't you, that the governors and mayors who imposed the

191 Atlas, Scott W. 2020. "The data is in—stop the panic and end the total isolation." *The Hill*, April 22; Reilly, Wilfred. 2020. "There is no empirical evidence for these lockdowns." *Spiked*, April 22; TOI Staff. 2020. "Top Israeli prof claims simple stats show virus plays itself out after 70 days." *Times of Israel*, April 14. ; Ellyat, Holly. 2020. "Sweden resisted a lockdown, and its capital Stockholm is expected to reach 'herd immunity' in weeks." *CNBC*, April 22; 2020. "Why a study showing that covid-19 is everywhere is good news." *The Economist*, April 11; Unherd. 2020. "Why lockdowns are the wrong policy - Swedish expert Prof. Johan Giesecke." *YouTube*, April 17; Paterlini, Marta. 2020. "'Closing borders is ridiculous': the epidemiologist behind Sweden's controversial Coronavirus strategy." *Nature*, April 21.

192 Magness, Phillip W. 2020. "Now It's Obvious: The Political Class and the Media Are Spinning Tales." *American Institute for Economic Research*, April 14.

lockdowns never asked their citizens about their views about instantly getting rid of all rights and freedoms. They didn't consult legislatures. They didn't consult a range of expert opinion or pay attention to any serious demographic data that showed how utterly preposterous it was to force non-vulnerable populations into house arrest while trapping vulnerable populations in nursing homes that became Covid-soaked killing fields.

They thought nothing of shattering business confidence, violating contractual rights, wrecking tens of millions of lives, prohibiting freedom in association, tanking the stock market, blowing all budgets, shutting down international travel, and even closing the churches. Amazing. Every government executive except a few became a tin-pot dictator.

The first hint of the possible blowback came from Henry Kissinger who warned in the *Wall Street Journal* on April 3, 2020:[193] "Nations cohere and flourish on the belief that their institutions can foresee calamity, arrest its impact and restore stability. When the Covid-19 pandemic is over, many countries' institutions will be perceived as having failed." Yes, that's quite an understatement.

From testing failures to policy failures to profligate fiscal and monetary policies to straight up brutalism in its shutdown antics, the reputation of government in general will not fare well. When the dust settles on this, a whole generation of leaders could be wiped out, provided we return to democratic forms of government, which surely we will. Left or right, Republican or Democrat, there will be a serious price to pay. Politicians acted rashly for fear of their political futures. They will find that they made the wrong choice.

3. Blowback Against Environmentalism

Wash your hands, they kept telling us. But we turn on the faucet and hardly anything comes out. They ruined them some years ago with flow stoppers. The water isn't hot because the hot-water heaters don't work as well due to regulations. Keep your clothing and dishes clean but our

193 Kissinger, Henry. 2020. "The Coronavirus Pandemic Will Forever Alter the World Order." *The Wall Street Journal*, April 3.

washing machines and dishwashers hardly work. And let us not forget that our toilets are also non-functional.

Government has wrecked sanitation by ruining our appliances in the name of conservation.[194] And now we suddenly discover that we care about cleanliness and getting rid of germs: nice discovery! Implementing this is going to require that we upend the restrictions, pull out the flow stoppers, permission new and functioning toilets, turn up our water heaters, fix the detergents and so on. We played fast and loose with germs and now we regret it.

So yes, plastic bags are back, and the disease-carrying reusables are gone, but that's just the beginning.[195] Recycling mandates will go away.[196] Hand dryers in bathrooms will be rethought.[197] Bring back single-use items and universalize them! We will care again about the quality of life as a first priority. As for nature and nature's germs, be gone!

4. Blowback Against Social Distance

Staying away from direct contact with sick people is a good idea; we've known since the ancient world. Vulnerable populations need to be especially careful which elderly people have always known. But government took this sensible idea and went crazy with it, separating everyone from everyone else, all in the name of "flattening the curve" to preserve hospital capacity. But then this principle became a general one, to the point that people were encouraged to believe silly things like that standing too close to anyone will magically cause Covid-19 to appear. Going to the grocery in 2020, it's pretty clear that people think you can get Covid-19 by talking or looking at people.

---

194 Tucker, Jeffrey A. 2018. "What Has Government Done to Our Bathrooms?" *American Institute for Economic Research*, January 10.

195 Flager, Madison. 2017. "Reuseable Shopping Bags Could Be Making You Sick." *Delish*, October 3.

196 Carden, Art. 2020. "Good Riddance to Recycling Trucks." *American Institute for Economic Research*, April 20.

197 Magness, Phillip W. 2020. "Rethink the Disease-Spreading Hand Dryer in a Pandemic." *American Institute for Economic Research*, March 23.

Several friends have pointed out to me that they already detect a blowback against all this. And why? There is a dubious merit to the overly generalized principle, and that will become more than obvious in the coming months. Then the blowback hits. I expect a widespread social closening movement to develop here pretty quickly. You will see the bars and dance floors packed, and probably a new baby boom will emerge in a post-Covid-19 world. And the handshake will again become what it began as, a sign of mutual trust.

5. Blowback Against Regulation

In the midst of panic, we discovered that many rules that govern our lives don't make sense. The regulations on disease testing clogged the system and gave us an epistemic crisis that kicked off this insanity in the first place.[198] Fortunately many politicians did the right thing and repealed many of them. The Americans for Tax Reform has assembled a list of 350 regulations that have been waived.[199] This is hugely encouraging. Let's keep them waived and never go back.

6. Blowback Against Digital Everything

We keep hearing how this trauma is going to cause everyone to communicate more with video. I don't believe it. Everyone is experiencing tremendous burnout of these sterile digital environments. Hey, it's great that they can happen but they are far from ideal.

"Can you hear me?"
"I can't hear you."
"Is my picture blurry?"
"Why am I looking up your nose?"
"Change your settings."
"Silence your mic!"

---

198 See article herein entitled, "An Epistemic Crisis."

199 Morales, Isabelle. 2020. "List: 380 Regulations Waived to Help Fight COVID-19." *Americans for Tax Reform*, April 24.

And so on. At first we thought this was merely a period of adjustment. Now we know that we just don't like all this nonsense. It's no way to live. There is nothing like real people in a real room.

7. Blowback Against Anti-Work

I suppose many workers weren't entirely unhappy when the boss said work from home. But millions of people have now discovered that this comes at a cost. There is loneliness. The dog. The kids. The spouse. The depressing failure to dress up like a civilized human being. Everyone I know misses the office. They want to be back, be on a schedule, see friends again, experience the joy of collaboration, share jokes, munch on the office donuts.

It was only recently that everyone seemed to be complaining about the workplace. There were endless squabbles about pay, pay equity, race, #metoo movements, executive compensation, family leave policies, and you name it. No one seemed happy. We didn't know how good we had it.

8. Blowback Against Experts

The media from the beginning trumpeted some experts over others. We went credential crazy. How many letters you have after your name determines your credibility (unless you have the wrong opinion). But soon we discovered some interesting realities. The experts that everyone wanted to cite were wrong or so loose with their predictions that their predictions were useless in practice.[200] Dr. Fauci himself wrote on February 28, 2020, that this would be a normal flu.[201] Merely a week later, everything changed from calm to panic, and with that change came the wild government response, long after people on their own realized that being careful would be a good idea. Under expert guidance, we swung from one end to the other with very little evidence, exactly against the strong and compelling

---

200 Magness, Phillip W. 2020. "How Wrong Were the Models and Why?" *American Institute for Economic Research*, April 23.

201 Fauci, Anthony S., H. Clifford Lane, & Robert R. Redfield. 2020. "Covid-19—Navigating the Uncharted." *New England Journal of Medicine*, 382: 1268-1269.

advice of one of the few experts with credibility remaining.[202]

9. Blowback Against Academia

Just like that, we went from enormously expensive campuses and a huge administrative apparatus to a series of Zoom calls between professor and students, leaving many to wonder what the rest is really worth. Surely many colleges and universities will not survive this. The other problem concerns the marketability of degrees in a world in which whole industries can be shut down in an instant. The college degree was supposed to give us security; the lockdowns took it all away. Also there is the problem of the curriculum itself. Of what value are these soft degrees in social justice in a world in which you are struggling to pay next month's rent regardless? As for elementary and secondary education, homeschooling anyone? It existed under a cloud for decades, before suddenly becoming mandatory.

10. Blowback Against Unhealthy Lifestyles

There has been no small effort to suppress the demographics of Covid-19 fatalities but the word is still getting out. This BBC headline sums it up: "Nine in 10 dying have existing illness."[203] And here's another: "Obesity is the number one factor in COVID deaths."[204] This should not be lost on people considering improving their overall health and reducing disease vulnerability. Maybe you already feel it and are using your quarantine time to get fit or at least stop advancing too quickly toward your final demise. There are things we can do, people! This would be an enormous change in American culture, to say the least.

11. Blowback Against Spending

You are likely saving lots of money from cutting entertainment. Feels good,

202 Stringham, Edward Peter. 2020. "Who Is John Ioannidis?" *American Institute for Economic Research*, April 19.

203 Triggle, Nick. 2020. "Coronavirus: Nine in 10 dying have existing illness." *BBC News*, April 16.

204 Sherman, Amy. 2020. "Is obesity a top risk factor in COVID-19 hospitalizations?" *Politifact*, April 17.

doesn't it? Regret not having saved more to prepare for these days? This will change dramatically. Those mattresses are going to get stuffed with cash in the coming year or two. It's all fine: savings leads to investment, provided people have an ironclad promise that nothing like the monstrous destruction of the past six months will ever occur again.

Monkey See, Monkey Do

A mystery for these many months is how so many governments in so many different places on earth could have adopted the same or very similar preposterous policies, no matter the threat level of the virus, and without firm evidence that interventions had any hope of being effective.

In the course of two weeks, traditional freedoms were zapped away in nearly all developed countries. In a seriously bizarre twist, even the silliest policies replicated themselves like a virus in country after country.

For example, you can't try on clothing in a store in Texas or in Melbourne, or in London or in Kalamazoo. What's with that? We know that the Covid-19 bug is least likely to live on fabrics unless I have symptoms of it, sneeze on my handkerchief and then I stuff it in your mouth.[205] The whole thing is a ridiculous mysophobic overreach, like most of the rules under which we live.

Then there was the inside/outside confusion. First everyone was forced indoors and people were arrested for being outdoors. Later, once restaurants started opening, people were not allowed indoors so eating establishments scrambled to make outdoor dining possible. Are we supposed to believe that the virus lived outside for a while but then later moved inside?

And curfews. So many places have them despite a complete absence of evidence that Covid-19 spread prefers the night to the day. I guess the real

---

205 Murphy, Alice. 2020. "Why you are LESS likely to catch COVID-19 from clothes (as long as you wash them): The everyday surfaces that leave you at risk for up to three days are revealed." *Daily Mail UK*, March 30.

point is to put a stop to revelry that might bring people together in a fun way? It's like all our governments decided on the same day that Covid-19 spreads through smiles and fun, so we have to banish both.

In Sydney and Los Angeles, and also in Detroit and Miami, you need to wear a mask when you walk in a restaurant but not when you sit. And this 6-foot rule is highly suspect too. It seems to imply that if you get too close to each other, Covid-19 spontaneously appears. At least people seem to believe that.

Australia, in its way, even created a slogan and a jingle to go with it. "Staying Apart Keeps Us Together," says Orwell, I mean, Victoria.[206]

Socially distance! Don't be a silent spreader! Even though the largest study yet has shown that "asymptomatic cases were least likely to infect their close contacts."[207] Which is to say, this is mostly nonsense.

In most places too, you have to quarantine two weeks when you arrive from afar, even though it is rare that the virus incubation period is that long. The mean period is 6 days, perhaps, which is what one would expect from a coronavirus like the common cold.[208]

Oh, and in department stores, you can't spray perfume to try it out, because surely that spreads Covid-19 – not. Except that there is not one shred of evidence that there is any truth to this. This one seems completely made up, though it is widely imposed.

The list goes on. The bans of gatherings over 50 people outdoors and 25 people indoors, the closures of gyms at a time when people need to be getting healthy, the shutting of theaters and bowling alleys but the keeping open of big-box stores – these policies are as ubiquitous as they are unsupported by any science. And we've known this for many months,

---

206 Green, Ricki. 2020. "Victorian Government Launches 'Staying Apart Keeps Us Together' Campaign Via M&C Saatchi." *Campaign Brief*, May 4.

207 Luo, Lei, Dan Lui, Xinlong Liao, Xianbo Wu. 2020. "Contact Settings and Risk for Transmission in 3410 Close Contacts of Patients With COVID-19 in Guangzhou, China." *Annals of Internal Medicine*, August 13.

208 Backer, Jantien A., Don Klinkenberg, and Jacco Wallinga. 2020. "Incubation period of 2019 novel coronavirus (2019-nCoV) infections among travellers from Wuhan, China, 20–28 January 2020 separator commenting unavailable." *Eurosurveillance*, 25(5).

ever since the media meltdown over Florida Spring Break ended up in zero fatal cases contracted at the revelry.

The worst case is school closings. They were shut down at the same time all over the world, despite evidence available since at least January that the threat to children is nearly zero. Yes, they do get Covid-19 almost entirely asymptomatically, which is to say they do not get "sick" in the old-fashioned sense of that term. What's more, they are highly unlikely to spread it to adults precisely because they do not have symptoms. This is widely admitted.[209]

Still governments decided to wreck kids' lives for an entire season.

And the timing of it all seems strangely suspicious. All these countries and states implemented this compulsory clown show at the same time, whether cases were everywhere or nowhere.

In the US, this was fascinating to watch. The shutdowns happened all over the country. In the Northeast, the virus had already spread widely toward herd immunity. The South shut down at the same time but the virus wasn't even there. By the time the virus did arrive, most states in the South had already reopened. The virus doesn't seem to care either way.

Now, looking at this it is very easy to go to conspiracy as the explanation. There is probably some secret hand at work somewhere that is guiding all of this, the thinking goes. How can so many governments in the world have simultaneously lost their marbles and abolished the people's liberties in such a cruel way, while trampling on all rights of property and association?

I tend to resist big conspiracy theories on this subject simply because I seriously doubt that governments are smart enough to implement them. From what I can see, these governors and statesmen seem to be making things up in a crazy panic and then sticking with them just to pretend that they know what they are doing.

Pete Earle's theory of pot commitment seems to explain why the stringency persists even in the lack of evidence that they do anything to

---

209 Fourcade, Marthe. 2020. "School Children Don't Spread Coronavirus, French Study Shows." *Bloomberg*, June 23.

suppress the virus.[210]

But how can we account for the imposition of so many similarly ridiculous rules at the same time across so many parts of the globe?

Rather than go full conspiracy, I invite you to examine a very interesting study published by the National Academy of Sciences: Explaining the homogeneous diffusion of Covid-19 nonpharmaceutical interventions across heterogeneous countries.[211]

A clearer title might be: how so many governments behaved so stupidly at once. The theory they posit seems highly realistic to me:

> We analyze the adoption of nonpharmaceutical interventions in the Organisation for Economic Co-operation and Development (OECD) countries during the early phase of the coronavirus disease 2019 (COVID-19) pandemic. Given the complexity associated with pandemic decisions, governments are faced with the dilemma of how to act quickly when their core decision-making processes are based on deliberations balancing political considerations. Our findings show that, in times of severe crisis, **governments follow the lead of others and base their decisions on what other countries do.** Governments in countries with a stronger democratic structure are slower to react in the face of the pandemic but are more sensitive to the influence of other countries. We provide insights for research on international policy diffusion and research on the political consequences of the COVID-19 pandemic.

This seems to fit with what I've seen anecdotally.

These guys in charge are mostly attorneys with specializations in

210 Earle, Peter C. 2020. "Intellectuals, Politicians, and Pot Commitment." *American Institute for Economic Research*, August 20.

211 Sebhatu, Abiel, Karl Wennberg, Stefan Arora-Jonsson, and Staffan I. Lindberg. 2020. "Explaining the homogeneous diffusion of COVID-19 nonpharmaceutical interventions across heterogeneous countries." *Proceedings of the National Academy of Sciences of the United States of America*, August 11.

bamboozling voters. And the "public health authorities" advising them can get credentials in the field without ever having studied – much less practiced – medicine. So what do they do? They copy other governments, as a way of covering up their ignorance.

As the study says:

> While our paper cannot judge what an "optimal" adoption timing would be for any country, it follows, from our findings of what appears to be **international mimicry** of intervention adoptions, that some countries may have adopted restrictive measures rather sooner than necessary. If that is the case, such countries may have incurred excessively high social and economic costs, and may experience problems sustaining restrictions for as long as is necessary due to lockdown fatigue.

Which is to say: the closures, lockdowns, and imposed stringency measures were not science. It was monkey see, monkey do. The social psychology experiments on conformity help explain this better than anything else.[212] They see some governments doing things and decide to do them too, as a way of making sure they are avoiding political risk, regardless of the cost.

All of which only increases one's respect for the governments around the world that did not lock down, did not close business, did not shut down schools, did not mandate masks, and did not push some crazy kabuki dance of social distancing in perpetuity. South Dakota, Sweden, Taiwan, and Belarus come to mind. It takes an unusual and rare level of incredulity to avoid this kind of herd mentality.

Why did so many governments go so nuts at once, disregarding their own laws, traditions, and values by bludgeoning their own people with the excuse of science that has turned out to be almost completely bogus? Some people claim conspiracy but a much simpler answer might be that, in their ignorance and stupor, they copied each other out of fear.

---

212 Press Books. "73. Conformity, Compliance, and Obedience." *Press Books.*

With that realization, too, comes some hope. If governments can copy each other in violating people's rights, they can copy each other in liberalization too. They can see how the liberal path is the one most consistent with building both health and wealth. Even if they do not, we all should. After all, the whole idea of government in the post-Enlightenment ideal is that it is the servant not the master of the population. With the ghastly experiences of 2020 in our minds, knowing what the coercive rule by bad science can do to our lives, we can and should reclaim that idea. Countries and societies that choose liberty over lockdown can thrive as never before.

We Need a Principled
Anti-Lockdown Movement

Shell-shocked is a good way to describe the mood in the US for a good part of the Spring of 2020. Most of us never thought it could happen here. I certainly did not, even though I've been writing about pandemic lockdown plans for 15 years. I knew the plans were on the shelf, which is egregious, but I always thought something would stop it from happening. The courts. Public opinion. Bill of Rights. Tradition. The core rowdiness of American culture. Political squeamishness. The availability of information.

Something would prevent it. So I believed. So most of us believed.

Still it happened, all in a matter of days, March 12-16, 2020 — and boom: it was over! We were locked down. Schools shut. Bars and restaurants closed. No international visitors. Theaters shuttered. Conferences forcibly ended. Sports stopped. We were told to stay home and watch movies... for two weeks to flatten the curve. Then those two weeks stretched into six months. How lucky for those who lived in the states that resisted the pressure and stayed open, but even they couldn't visit relatives in other states due to quarantine requirements and travel restrictions.

Lockdowns ended American life as we knew it just six months ago, for a virus: that 99.4-6% of those who contract it shake off; for which the median age of death is 78-80 with comorbidities; for which there is not a single verified case of reinfection on the planet; for which international successes in managing this relied on herd immunity and openness.[213] Still the politicians who had become dictators couldn't admit such astonishing failure, so they kept the restrictions in place as a way of covering up what they had done.

That shock of Spring turned to a Summer of wickedness, with everyone pointing fingers at everyone else for the sorry state of life. Patience has run out and a national viciousness has taken its place. It is evident not only online but in person where strangers scream at each other for behaving in ways in which they disapprove. America became an extremely ugly place. This is what lockdowns did.

What many states are called "open" today would have been called "closed" six months previously. Sports were rare. Theaters weren't open. In some places, you still cannot go to gyms or eat inside. Mask mandates were everywhere, and mask enforcers too. People ratted out their neighbors, sent drones to ferret out house parties, and lashed out at each other in public places.

In a mere six months, lockdowners manufactured a new form of social structure in which everyone is expected to treat everyone else as a deadly contagion. Even more preposterously, people have come to believe that if you come within six feet of another person, a disease spontaneously appears and spreads.

All of this has occurred in the midst of the greatest political divide in many generations. Oddly, you can almost predict a person's political allegiance based on their attitude toward the virus, as if sitting political figures are responsible for creating or controlling pathogens that have been part of the human experience since we first walked and talked. The politicization of Covid-19 has been a terrible noise that has distracted from wise disease management that characterized the American way for more than a century.

But the American people support this, right? I've never been sure. It's

---

213 Meyerowitz-Katz, Gideon, and Lea Merone. 2020. "A systematic review and meta-analysis of published research data on COVID-19 infection-fatality rates." *MedRxiv*, July 7; CDC. 2020. "Characteristics of Persons Who Died with COVID-19 — United States, February 12–May 18, 2020." *CDC*, July 17; Mandavilli, Apoorva. 2020. "Can You Get Covid-19 Again? It's Very Unlikely, Experts Say." *The New York Times*, July 22; Worldometer. 2020. "Sweden: Coronavirus Cases." *Worldometer*.

true that the TV and online media are blaring panic all day every day. If that's where you get your information, it certainly must feel like a plague. There is also the problem that people feel tremendously powerless right now. They have been locked down, silenced, humiliated, brutalized. The few attempts to get out and protest the lockdowns were greeted with jeers and derision by mainstream media. But it turned out that this was because they were protesting the wrong thing. When the protests against police brutality and racism swept the country, the media wholly approved. Yes, it all felt like gaslighting.[214]

Where precisely does American opinion stand on lockdowns today? One cannot trust the polls: people know exactly what they are supposed to say to pollsters during a police-state lockdown. It's usually a good guess that one-third of Americans take a position that is more-or-less consistent with human liberty – it's not a fixed group and it shifts depending on the issue – so that's probably a good guess now.

The incredible frenzy of the misinforming media has confused vast numbers. A poll revealed that many Americans think that 9% of us have died from Covid-19 whereas it is really 0.04%. So yes, we have a propaganda problem, starting with the *New York Times*, which in early August demanded "more aggressive shutdowns than have been carried out in the past.[215] The United States has not had a true national lockdown, shuttering only about half the country, compared with 90 percent in other countries with more successful outbreak control."

None of which is true. The proportion of people who are saying true things seem to be only 1% in comparison with the barrage of media-culture nonsense. We see almost no discussion in the mainstream press of empirical evidence at home and abroad that the lockdowns make no sense from a medical and economic perspective.[216] Medical experts for

---

214 Breashears, Caroline. 2020. "The Gaslighting of the American People." *American Institute for Economic Research*, August 6.

215 The Editorial Board. 2020. "America Could Control the Pandemic by October. Let's Get to It." *The New York Times*, August 8.

216 Tucker, Jeffrey A. 2020. "The Virus Doesn't Care about Your Policies." *American Institute for Economic Research*, July 31.

many decades have warned against disturbing social functioning in the event of disease. Preserving freedom has always been the policy priority: 1949-52, 1957-58, 1968-69, and 2005.[217] The American Revolution itself took place in the midst of a smallpox outbreak.[218] Liberalism arose during centuries of pandemics.[219]

And yet here we are.

This country needs a serious anti-lockdown movement, one that is not just political but cultural and intellectual, one that is deeply educated on history, philosophy, law, economics, and all sciences, and can rally around traditional American civic postulates concerning individual freedom and the limits of governments, and also around universal principles of human rights. If liberty means anything, it means that we are not locked down. It means, moreover, that lockdowns are unconscionable.

What should this movement – which need not be formally organized – study, believe, and teach?

Because property rights are the first rights to be violated in lockdown, the movement needs to embrace and champion the right of private ownership and control: of businesses, homes, and ourselves. The liberal tradition has long affirmed this principle, and it is nothing but appalling that the lockdowns took place as if private property doesn't exist. Suddenly everything and everyone belonged to the state, and it would be the state to declare what is – or is not – essential, or even what is elective vs. non-elective for your medical care.

It should embrace the freedom to choose our associations, since that is what came under attack next: we couldn't gather in groups, hold conferences, go to the movies, do anything considered not "socially distant" (I'm so sick of that phrase that I can barely type it), or even go to another state to visit friends and relatives.

217 Tucker, Jeffrey A. 2020. "A Retrospective on the Avian Flu Scare of 2005." *American Institute for Economic Research*, March 22.

218 Tucker, Jeffrey A. 2020. "The American Revolution Occurred in the Middle of a Pandemic." *American Institute for Economic Research*, July 4.

219 Murphy, Jon. 2020. "Liberalism Was Born and Grew During Centuries of Pandemics." *American Institute for Economic Research*, May 26.

This movement needs to celebrate and defend religious freedom, since, incredibly, most houses of worship were forcibly closed by government. The modern idea of freedom came about in the late Middle Ages when exhaustion from religious wars gradually gave rise to the idea of tolerance. Religious toleration was the first great freedom that came to be codified in law. It's stunning that it was so flagrantly violated this year.

This movement must come to terms with free enterprise and the innovation that comes with it. How much wealth and creativity has been lost in the lockdowns? It's unfathomable. The biggest victims have been small- and medium-sized businesses, whereas the large tech firms have thrived. To start and manage a commercial enterprise is a human right, the realization of which was the great achievement of modern life, as it spread prosperity throughout the world and lifted up the world's people from the state of nature to levels of the entrenched hierarchies of old.

Part of this liberal ideal is free trade, which has in recent years come under fire from both the left and right. Don't forget that Donald Trump kicked off this dictatorial frenzy with his sudden and shocking bans of travel from China and Europe, which resulted in a frantic mass crowding of airports in the days following. He did it with a stroke of a pen, overriding all his advisors. He still brags about it.

How much did his extreme reaction here inspire governors to do the same? Of course Trump's actions reflect his persistent preference for isolationism on not only trade but immigration too. Even now, Trump is refusing to allow foreign workers into the US (except for emergency cases) because he incorrectly believes this will help the American job market. It's an outrage: free enterprise entitles the employment of anyone from anywhere. This is a policy that is indisputably good for everyone.

So long as we are talking about freedom fundamentals, let's talk about masks. They have become exactly what the *New England Journal of Medicine* called them: a talisman.[220] They are symbols of social commitment and political loyalty. A free society rallies around individual choice, so if masks

---

220 Klompas, Michael, Charles A. Morris, Julia Sinclair, Madelyn Pearson, and Erica S. Shenoy. 2020. "Universal Masking in Hospitals in the Covid-19 Era." *The New England Journal of Medicine*, 382:e63.

make a person feel safe, or if it makes them feel they are keeping others safe from their breath, fine. But when people attack others for resisting wearing them, and are apparently upset at the seeming appearance of rebellion from rules, this is imposition and intolerance – perhaps understandable given the times, but still illiberal.

Laws requiring face coverings in public would never have been tolerated even six months ago. And yet here we are, not only with laws but a growing number of recruits within the public to enforce them with appalling rudeness. It's hardly the first time in history. American sumptuary laws in Colonial times mandated that people not dress in fancy clothes for reasons of piety and social conformism. Part of the capitalist revolution included the freedom to dress as one wants and the mass availability of fashion for everyone. The mandatory mask movement and its shock troops among the public is but a revival of puritanism.

The lockdowns crushed the economic prospects of millions, and government attempted to make up for that with wild spending of other people's money and an unprecedented use of the printing press, as if government can somehow paper over the destruction it caused. Therefore, the anti-lockdown movement needs a commitment to fiscal sanity and sound money. We now know that a government with the capacity to create unlimited amounts of paper money cannot be constrained. This needs to be fixed.

As for health, the topic or excuse that unleashed the lockdowns in the first place, we surely should learn from this experience that politics and medicine need to be separated with a high wall. We have medical professionals who are traditionally in charge of mitigating disease, and they do so in line with their own professional associations and best judgement. Politics should never override the doctor/patient relationship, nor presume to know what is better for us than our own physicians.

On the matter of education, governors all over the country cruelly locked down all the schools, though there is near-zero threat to kids from the virus and there is, after six months, still no verified case of a child passing Covid-19 to an adult.[221] Perhaps a small silver lining is that we have learned more about how parents can exercise more control over education than they have previously had. The anti-lockdown movement needs to embrace a multiplicity of educational alternatives including the possibility of full privatization so that education can again be part of the free enterprise matrix.

It's true that anti-lockdown carries a negative connotation. Is there a better word to convey the positive dimension? My preference: liberalism. Progressives have abandoned it. It is also correct from a historical and international perspective. Liberalism and modernity are inextricably linked in history, says Benjamin Constant.[222] A liberalism of the future needs to be prepared to understand, advocate, and fight for freedom in a non-lockdown world. No exceptions.

This takes us to the final point. Whether this movement is working in the realms of academia, culture, journalism, or politics, there is an absolute urgency that it exercize unrelenting moral courage and integrity. Ferociously. It should be uncompromising on crucial points. It must be willing to speak even when it is unfashionable to do so, even when the media is screaming the opposite, even when the Twitter mob floods your notifications, even when you are shamed for thinking for yourself.

This time around, as you have surely noticed, even the voices of good people with good ideas fell silent in fear. This fear must be banished. The blowback against this despotism will come but it is not enough. We need character, integrity, courage, and truth, and this perhaps matters more than ideology and knowledge. Knowledge without the willingness and courage to speak is useless, because (as E.C. Harwood taught us) for integrity there is no substitute.

In the end, the case for unlocking society is a spiritual matter. What is your life worth and how do you want to live it? How important are the hard-won freedoms you exercise daily? What of the lives and liberties

---

221 Griffiths, Sian. 2020. "'Pupils pose little risk of spreading Covid.'" *The Times*, August 9.

222 Wikipedia. 2020. "The Liberty of Ancients Compared with that of Moderns." *Wikipedia*, June 29.

of others? These are everything. Freedom has never prevailed without passionate and courageous voices to defend it. We have the tools now, many more than before. They can throttle us but can't finally shut us down. The notion that we would fail to speak for fear of the Twitter mob is absurd.

This movement, whether it is called anti-lockdown or just plain liberalism, must reject the wickedness and compulsion of this current moment in American life. It needs to counter the brutalism of lockdowns.[223] It needs to speak and act with humane understanding and high regard for social functioning under freedom, and the hope for the future that comes with it. The enemies of freedom and human rights have revealed themselves for the world to see. Let there be justice. The well-being of us all is at stake.

---

223 Tucker, Jeffrey A. 2020. "The Return of Brutalism." *American Institute for Economic Research*, June 15.

About the Author

Jeffrey A. Tucker is president and founder of Brownstone Institute. He is the author of many thousands of articles in the scholarly and popular press and eight books in 5 languages. He speaks widely on topics of economics, technology, social philosophy, and culture, and writes a daily column on economics for Epoch Times.

About the Publisher

The Brownstone Institute is a nonprofit 501(c)(3) organization founded May 2021. Its vision is of a society that places the highest value on the voluntary interaction of individuals and groups while minimizing the use of violence and force including that which is exercised by public or private authorities. This vision is that of the Enlightenment which elevated learning, science, progress, and universal rights to the forefront of public life. It is constantly threatened by ideologies and systems that would take the world back to before the triumph of the ideal of freedom.

The motive force of Brownstone Institute was the global crisis created by policy responses to the Covid-19 pandemic of 2020. That trauma revealed a fundamental misunderstanding alive in all countries around the world today, a willingness on the part of the public and officials to relinquish freedom and fundamental human rights in the name of managing a public health crisis, which was not managed well in most countries. The consequences were devastating and will live in infamy.

INDEX

Made in United States
Orlando, FL
06 December 2023

40330241R00127